DISEASES & DISORDERS

Strokes

Robert Taylor

LUCENT BOOKS

An imprint of Thomson Gale, a part of The Thomson Corporation

THOMSON
™
GALE

Detroit • New York • San Francisco • New Haven, Conn. • Waterville, Maine • London

© 2007 Thomson Gale, a part of The Thomson Corporation.

Thomson and Star Logo are trademarks and Gale and Lucent Books are registered trademarks used herein under license.

For more information, contact:
Lucent Books
27500 Drake Rd.
Farmington Hills, MI 48331-3535
Or you can visit our Internet site at http://www.gale.com

LIBRARY OF CONGRESS CATALOGING-IN-PUBLICATION DATA

Taylor, Robert, 1948–
Strokes / by Robert Taylor.
    p. cm. — (Diseases and disorders)
Includes bibliographical references and index.
ISBN-13: 978-1-59018-967-2 (hardcover : alk. paper)
ISBN-10: 1-59018-967-1 (hardcover : alk. paper)
1. Cerebrovascular disease—Juvenile literature.   I. Title.
RC388.5T388 2007
616.8'1—dc22

                                                          2006018979

Printed in the United States of America

Table of Contents

"The Most Difficult Puzzles Ever Devised"

Charles Best, one of the pioneers in the search for a cure for diabetes, once explained what it is about medical research that intrigued him so. "It's not just the gratification of knowing one is helping people," he confided, "although that probably is a more heroic and selfless motivation. Those feelings may enter in, but truly, what I find best is the feeling of going toe to toe with nature, of trying to solve the most difficult puzzles ever devised. The answers are there somewhere, those keys that will solve the puzzle and make the patient well. But how will those keys be found?"

Since the dawn of civilization, nothing has so puzzled people—and often frightened them, as well—as the onset of illness in a body or mind that had seemed healthy before. A seizure, the inability of a heart to pump, the sudden deterioration of muscle tone in a small child—being unable to reverse such conditions or even to understand why they occur was unspeakably frustrating to healers. Even before there were names for such conditions, even before they were understood at all, each was a reminder of how complex the human body was, and how vulnerable.

While our grappling with understanding diseases has been frustrating at times, it has also provided some of humankind's most heroic accomplishments. Alexander Fleming's accidental discovery in 1928 of a mold that could be turned into penicillin has resulted in the saving of untold millions of lives. The isolation of the enzyme insulin has reversed what was once a death sentence for anyone with diabetes. There have been great strides in combating conditions for which there is not yet a cure, too. Medicines can help AIDS patients live longer, diagnostic tools such as mammography and ultrasounds can help doctors find tumors while they are treatable, and laser surgery techniques have made the most intricate, minute operations routine.

This "toe-to-toe" competition with diseases and disorders is even more remarkable when seen in a historical continuum. An astonishing amount of progress has been made in a very short time. Just two hundred years ago, the existence of germs as a cause of some diseases was unknown. In fact, it was less than 150 years ago that a British surgeon named Joseph Lister had difficulty persuading his fellow doctors that washing their hands before delivering a baby might increase the chances of a healthy delivery (especially if they had just attended to a diseased patient)!

Each book in Lucent's Diseases and Disorders series explores a disease or disorder and the knowledge that has been accumulated (or discarded) by doctors through the years. Each book also examines the tools used for pinpointing a diagnosis, as well as the various means that are used to treat or cure a disease. Finally, new ideas are presented—techniques or medicines that may be on the horizon.

Frustration and disappointment are still part of medicine, for not every disease or condition can be cured or prevented. But the limitations of knowledge are being pushed outward constantly; the "most difficult puzzles ever devised" are finding challengers every day.

INTRODUCTION

Sudden Tragedy

Stroke occurs suddenly. The disease used to be called apoplexy, a Greek word meaning "to strike down," because it attacks individuals without warning. Victims report feeling fine one second and being inexplicably unable to talk or walk the next. Strokes affect the brain, damaging the most complex organ in the human body and impairing any of a variety of motor and cognitive skills controlled by it.

The brain controls many functions—perception, movement, emotion, thought. It is also the seat of the personality. When it is damaged, as it is when a stroke happens, the victim is changed. In some cases, a stroke victim's personality is altered forever by the damage done to the brain or by the frustrating struggle to recover from disabilities caused by the stroke. In other instances, motor skills or speech are impaired. People who once worked with their hands may discover they can no longer control the movements of their fingers. People whose livelihood depended on their ability to speak clearly and forcefully to others find they can no longer communicate. Athletes lose their strength and coordination. Parents are robbed of their ability to care for their families. Stroke is a life-changing disease.

Author Eric Hodgins describes how a stroke turned him from a fully functioning person to a helpless medical statistic

6

in a matter of minutes. He was chatting on the telephone when he suffered a stroke. He says:

> To my shock and incredulity, I could not speak. That is, I could utter nothing intelligible. All that would come from my lips was the sound ah, which I repeated again and again. . . . Then as I watched it, the telephone hand piece slid slowly from my grasp, and I, in turn, slid slowly from my chair and landed on the floor behind the desk. . . . At 5:15 in that January dusk I had been a person; now, at 6:45 I was a case.[1]

Two-thirds of stroke victims are age sixty-five or older, and more women die as a result of stroke than men.

Hodgins's case is one among many. Statistics reveal that stroke is a common disease. Someone in the United States has a stroke every forty-five seconds; more than half a million Americans become stroke victims every year, and 150,000 of those die as a result. Stroke is the third leading cause of death in the United States and the chief cause of disability. At present, approximately 3 million Americans are struggling with disabilities due to strokes.

Two-thirds of the victims are age sixty-five or older. More men than women are affected, but more women die as a result of suffering a stroke. There is no consensus on why, but African Americans are especially vulnerable. The human toll is devastating; the financial cost is also significant. Stroke drains more than $30 billion a year from the economy in medical expenses and lost worker productivity.

Despite these alarming statistics, stroke is less understood by the general public than any other major disease. Surveys indicate that most people do not know what causes strokes, what the risk factors are, or how the disease can be prevented. Medical specialists insist that the number of stroke cases would drop dramatically if people were more aware of the lifestyle factors that put them at risk.

Although there have been encouraging advances in the diagnosis and treatment of stroke, more people are expected to suffer the sudden life-altering effects of the disease in the years to come. Stroke is primarily, but not exclusively, a disease of old age. As more and more people live longer due to improved prevention and treatment of other diseases, the number of stroke cases will inevitably rise. Public-health officials are concerned that unless public awareness also increases, the instant tragedy of stroke will become a national health crisis.

CHAPTER ONE

What Is a Stroke?

A stroke is the sudden death of brain cells due to insufficient blood supply. Blood carries oxygen and nutrients to the body's cells. When something happens to disrupt the flow of blood, the cells in the deprived area are damaged. In extreme cases, the damage is extensive enough to cause death. The effects of a stroke depend on the location and size of the part of the brain starved of blood and how long the blood supply has been interrupted.

There are two broad classifications of stroke: ischemic and hemorrhagic. An ischemic stroke occurs when the blood supply to the brain is cut off or severely diminished by a blockage in an artery, one of the vessels that carry blood from the heart to other parts of the body. A hemorrhagic stroke happens when a vessel ruptures, preventing blood from reaching its destination. In both cases, the result is the same: the death of brain cells and temporary or permanent loss of the physical or mental capacities those brain cells made possible.

How the Brain Works

To understand strokes, it is first necessary to understand how the brain functions. The brain is an extremely complex organ. In the average adult human, it weighs about 3 pounds (1.36kg). It is made up of billions of cells, called neurons,

The Structure of the Brain

Side view

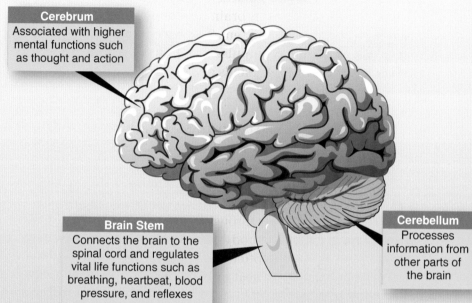

Cerebrum
Associated with higher mental functions such as thought and action

Brain Stem
Connects the brain to the spinal cord and regulates vital life functions such as breathing, heartbeat, blood pressure, and reflexes

Cerebellum
Processes information from other parts of the brain

Top view

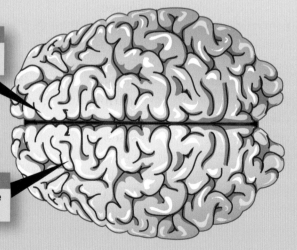

Right Hemisphere
Controls activity on the left side of the body

Left Hemisphere
Controls activity on the right side of the body

which communicate with each other in complicated ways, allowing people to walk, talk, think, and do all the other things associated with being alive. Along with the spinal column, the brain forms the body's central nervous system. Messages pass constantly between the brain and other parts of the body along pathways in the system. These messages, in the form of tiny electrochemical impulses, tell muscles to contract or relax and regulate how glands and organs operate.

Parts of the Brain

The brain is divided into compartments, each with its own special function. The brain stem, located right on top of the spinal column at the back of the head, governs automatic bodily activities like breathing, the rate at which the heart beats, eye movement, and quick reflex actions. The brain stem also contains the major pathway through which other parts of the brain communicate with the body. If this part of the brain is damaged by a stroke, death often results, because the victim's heart may lose the ability to beat or his or her lungs may no longer be able to breathe.

The cerebellum, found at the lower back of the brain just above the brain stem, functions like a computer, coordinating the activity of other parts of the brain. A stroke that affects this region has very serious consequences both for the victim's ability to move and for his or her ability to think and speak.

The cerebrum, which runs from the cerebellum to the front of the skull, is the largest part of the brain. It receives information from other parts of the body, analyzes it, compares it with previously stored information, and sends a message to the muscles if it decides action needs to be taken. This is the area of the brain that enables people to make decisions based on the memory of previous experience, one of the higher brain functions often said to distinguish humanity from other animals. "The cerebrum defines us as humans,"[2] says Dr. Vladimir Hachinski, a professor of neurology at the University of Western Ontario in Canada.

The cerebrum is divided into two hemispheres. The right hemisphere controls activity on the left side of the body; the left hemisphere governs behavior on the body's right side. When a stroke damages part of this region of the brain, the effects are usually felt only on one side of the body. If the cerebrum is damaged by a stroke, the patient can lose the ability to speak, understand speech, think logically, recognize visual patterns and relationships, remember, and control his or her emotions. In some cases, blindness results, usually in one eye, though the eye itself is perfectly healthy.

A stroke in the cerebrum can have bizarre consequences. In the seventeenth century, a thirty-three-year-old Swedish man suddenly lost his ability to speak. Yet, when he went to church, he could sing hymns without difficulty. His friends and family thought he was faking, and his religious friends thought his capacity to sing praises to God was evidence of a miracle. Today, doctors know he suffered a stroke that destroyed the speech center in left side of his brain. The right side of the brain has minimal speech potential, but it is highly attuned to music; hence, the man was able to sing, but not speak. Although the brain is divided into specialized compartments, those compartments do communicate with each other, accounting for the wide range and severity of stroke symptoms.

Blood Supply

Since a stroke occurs when the flow of blood to the brain is interrupted, it is necessary to understand precisely how blood, and the life-sustaining nutrients it contains, normally reaches the brain.

Four arteries supply blood to the brain. The two carotid arteries run along each side of the neck and are the main blood vessels that feed into the brain. Each of the carotid arteries divides into an internal carotid that goes straight into the brain and an external carotid that supplies the face and scalp. The point at which the divide occurs, called the bifurcation, is especially vulnerable to disease and damage. It is frequently the site of atherosclerosis, a hardening of the arteries that occurs when fatty deposits build up on the walls of the blood vessels and become solid. Atherosclerosis can cut off the brain's principal source of blood.

Blood Supply to the Brain

Two pairs of arteries, the carotid and the vertebral, supply blood to the brain. Blockages in these arteries can prevent blood flow to the brain and cause a stroke.

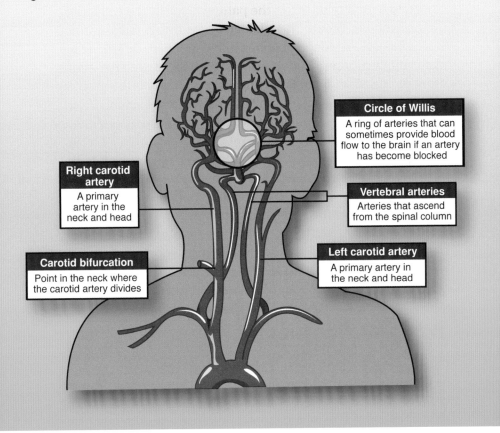

Circle of Willis
A ring of arteries that can sometimes provide blood flow to the brain if an artery has become blocked

Right carotid artery
A primary artery in the neck and head

Vertebral arteries
Arteries that ascend from the spinal column

Carotid bifurcation
Point in the neck where the carotid artery divides

Left carotid artery
A primary artery in the neck and head

The two vertebral arteries run inside the spine and join at the base of the brain to form a single artery. They help the carotid arteries nourish the brain, especially the cerebellum and the rear part of the cerebrum. At the base of the brain, at the top of the neck, the carotid and vertebral arteries join to form an anatomical structure called the circle of Willis, named after the scientist who discovered it. If one of the arteries fails to do its job in supplying blood to the brain, the others involved in the circle of Willis try to take up the slack. Usually, this is enough to prevent a stroke, but sometimes the flow of blood is so severely interrupted that a stroke will occur.

Blood not only delivers oxygen to the brain, it also carries sugar in the form of glucose that provides cells with energy. "Glucose is the only fuel normally used by brain cells," says Dr. Norberto Coimbra of the faculty of medicine at the University of São Paulo in Brazil. "Because neurons [brain cells] cannot store glucose, they depend on the bloodstream to deliver a constant supply of this precious fuel. . . . Brain cells need two times more energy than the other cells in your body."[3] If the glucose supply is cut off, brain cells begin to suffer immediately.

Ischemic Strokes

The brain's supply of blood and glucose can be interrupted in one of two ways: when an artery becomes blocked or when it ruptures. Thus, there are two main types of stroke, called ischemic and hemorrhagic, respectively. In general, an ischemic stroke occurs when the supply of blood to the brain is cut off by a clot in one of the arteries supplying the organ. A hemorrhagic stroke, on the other hand, happens when a vessel in the brain ruptures and blood it was carrying flows uselessly—and sometimes harmfully—into the tissue surrounding the brain and not the brain itself, the organ it was destined to nourish. In both cases, brain cells, starved of the nutrition they need, die. Once they are dead, they cannot be revived.

Eighty percent of all strokes are ischemic in nature. Blood clots form for a variety of reasons. Thrombosis is a term that describes a clot that occurs in one of the arteries directly feeding the brain. Most commonly, the artery becomes narrowed due to atherosclerosis. Blood flow slows down in the narrowed part of the artery and becomes stagnant. In a short time, a clot will form in the stagnant blood. A clot is a solid mass, and if it is big enough it will block the artery, reducing blood flow to zero. The brain cells depending on blood from that artery will be deprived of oxygen and glucose and will die in minutes if the blood flow is not restored.

A clot can also form elsewhere in the body and travel to one of the arteries supplying the brain. In this case, it is called an embolism. Embolisms have four main sources: the heart, the aorta (the major artery leading away from the heart), a neck

World Leaders Who Were Stroke Victims

A number of influential twentieth-century world leaders were victims of stroke. Woodrow Wilson, president of the United States from 1913 to 1921, suffered a series of strokes that left him unable to speak clearly. His wife became his spokesperson during the final years of his administration. In Russia, revolutionary leader Vladimir Lenin also had to rely on his wife to help him run the country when he was felled by a stroke in 1922.

All three leaders—American president Franklin Roosevelt, Russian premier Joseph Stalin, and British prime minister Winston Churchill—who convened at Yalta to determine the course of history after World War II had suffered strokes before their meeting. Roosevelt eventually died of a subsequent stroke.

President Dwight Eisenhower had a stroke that left him with slurred speech during his term of office between 1952 and 1960, and Richard Nixon died of a stroke twenty years after he resigned from the White House in 1974.

Churchill, Roosevelt, and Stalin (seated, from left) all survived strokes during their time as world leaders.

artery, or an artery in the leg. Clots, whether they are due to thrombosis or embolism, usually block only one artery feeding the brain. Consequently, the reduction of blood supply and the subsequent cell death is most often confined to one side of the brain.

Although atherosclerosis is responsible for most ischemic strokes, clots can also form in arteries that have been damaged due to injury. In these cases, which account for a large number of strokes experienced by younger people, the trauma of the injury can cause an artery to collapse partially, narrowing it and creating conditions where blood can stagnate and form a clot. Clots can also form in arteries that have been damaged

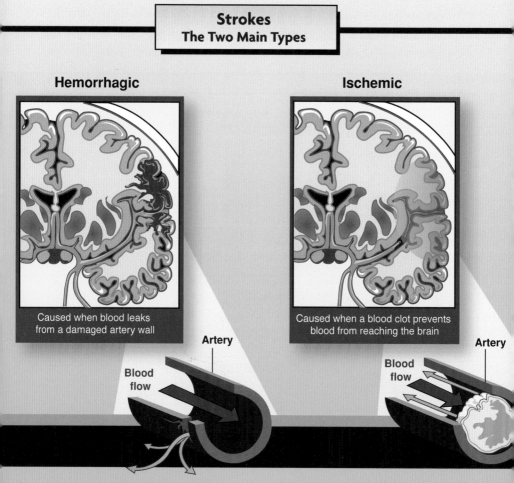

Strokes
The Two Main Types

Hemorrhagic

Caused when blood leaks from a damaged artery wall

Artery

Blood flow

Ischemic

Caused when a blood clot prevents blood from reaching the brain

Artery

Blood flow

by diseases like high blood pressure and diabetes. Clots can even be caused by abnormalities of the blood itself. Chemical imbalances, for example, can lead to an oversupply of chemicals produced by the body that encourage the blood to clot. In other cases, an insufficiency of the chemicals that promote the free flow of blood can have the same effect.

Hemorrhagic Stroke

Hemorrhagic strokes have the same consequences as ischemic strokes, but they are not caused by blood clotting. A hemorrhagic stroke occurs when a blood vessel bursts inside the brain. This may happen if the vessel is weakened by age or disease or sustains an injury, following, for example, a severe blow to the head. This type of stroke not only interrupts blood flow to certain brain cells, it also causes the discharged blood to accumulate, exerting pressure on other parts of the brain. This swelling is called cerebral edema. The tissue surrounding the accumulation of blood tries to resist the pressure it is exerting. Eventually, the blood coagulates into a mass called a hematoma, which compresses and displaces normal brain tissue. It can also squeeze other blood vessels, further reducing the amount of blood available to nourish brain cells. If the hematoma is large enough, it can be fatal.

Bleeding from the broken vessel can occur inside the brain itself, between two membranes that surround the entire brain, or between the outer membrane and the skull. Bleeding into the brain is called an intracerebral hemorrhage. It is the most serious of the three conditions because it damages the brain directly, disrupting the organ's delicate structure—often beyond repair. It is most frequently caused by high blood pressure, blood abnormalities, deformation of the arteries, trauma, or an excess of amyloid, a chemical associated with the brain-wasting condition known as Alzheimer's disease.

When the bleeding occurs between the two membranes surrounding the brain, it is called a subarachnoid hemorrhage. It is most often caused by an aneurysm, a weakening of the wall of a blood vessel. The cause of this weakening remains a medical mystery. Other factors that can lead to subarachnoid hemorrhages include head injury and malformation of the blood vessels. If the bleeding is between the outer membrane and the skull, it is a subdural hemorrhage. The most likely cause is head trauma. In these two cases, the symptoms are often general rather than specific because the pressure is exerted over the entire brain and not confined to one area. Rather than lose the ability to speak, for example, the victim may experience fatigue, confusion, loss of balance, and weakness.

Hemorrhagic strokes account for about 20 percent of all stroke cases, but they are as serious as ischemic strokes and often more difficult to treat since repairing the ruptured blood vessel may require delicate brain surgery, which involves many risks and can lead to additional brain damage. Case histories reveal how terrifying a hemorrhagic stroke can be.

A Thirteen-Year-Old's Ordeal

Hemorrhagic strokes and ischemic strokes have similar consequences. Although most strokes occur in older people, youngsters are not immune from the disease, especially hemorrhagic strokes, which are often caused by injury. A thirteen-year-old girl identified as Erica reports how a stroke caused by a broken blood vessel transformed her life.

Erica had been shopping with her mother when she developed a severe pain on the right side of her head. "It felt as though a knife had pierced my skull and sliced right through my brain," she says. "I started to scream because the pain in my head was so intense and unrelenting."[4]

Erica's mother called a neighbor, who was a doctor. He dismissed the girl's pleas for help as an overdramatic bid for attention, but he consented to drive her to the nearest emergency room. There, the physicians quickly concluded that she had overdosed on drugs. Only after extensive tests did they admit she had suffered an aneurysm and order her transported to another hospital for surgery. During the trip, she lost consciousness. Erica wrote:

My next memory is waking up days later. I was paralyzed on my left side, and I could not talk. No one in the room knew I could hear them. I heard the doctor telling my parents I would never walk again. I had no idea what they were talking about or where I was. I did not know that I had suffered three strokes. I had brain damage; enough to lead my doctors and family to believe I would never go on to lead a normal life.[5]

It took seven years of intensive therapy for Erica to recover from her ordeal. The only effect remaining is a slight abnormality in the pupil of her left eye. "I am glad that I know I have faced adversity and overcome it,"[6] she says.

Ischemic Nightmare

Ischemic strokes have equally devastating consequences. A forty-six-year-old nurse, who identifies herself as Debra, tells the dramatic story of her ischemic stroke. She was in the

Through intensive physical therapy, stroke victims such as this man may recover mobility lost to stroke.

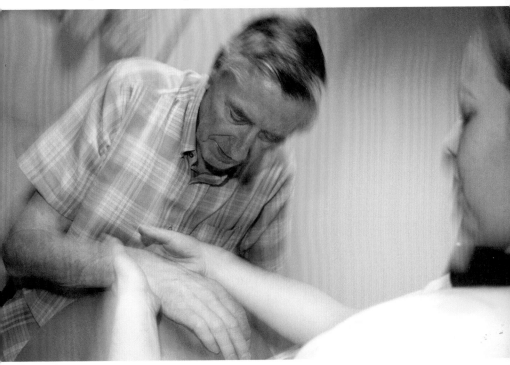

Systemic Hypoperfusion

Apart from strokes caused by blocked or bleeding arteries, a third type of stroke can occur when the heart cannot pump enough blood to nourish the brain. This condition is called systemic hypoperfusion, and it accounts for a relatively small number of strokes. Unlike ischemic and hemorrhagic strokes, strokes caused by systemic hypoperfusion affect both sides of the body. "Systemic hypoperfusion leads to more diffuse abnormalities such as light-headedness, dizziness, confusion, dimming of vision, and reduced hearing," says Dr. Louis Caplan in his book *Stroke*. "Patients appear pale and generally weak." This type of stroke can happen during a heart attack, congestive heart failure, or following an injury that results in excessive loss of blood. Treatment of strokes due to systemic hypoperfusion focuses on alleviating the underlying condition so that proper blood flow to the brain can be restored.

Louis R. Caplan, *Stroke*. St. Paul, MN: AAN, 2006, p. 19.

---

shower at 5:30 in the morning, thinking about a conference she had to attend at work, when she began to feel a hollow sensation in her skull. Debra says:

> I noticed I could not grasp anything with my left hand and suddenly I fell to the floor. As I lay there, trying to get up, the entire left side of my body was immobile and no matter how hard I tried my body simply did not respond to the commands. I found myself saying: "This can't be happening to me, people at 46 don't have strokes, just too young for a stroke. These kinds of things happen to other people, not to me."[7]

On her way to the hospital, Debra was haunted by one thought. "My life was never going to be as I knew it," she says. "Suddenly I was thrust into the role of a patient and out of my comfort zone of being in charge. I became totally dependent on others for even my most basic needs. . . . Never had others been allowed to see me cry and yet here I was unable to stop the flow."[8]

It took almost a year for Debra to learn to move the fingers of her left hand. After three years of therapy, she is still disabled and unable to work as a nurse. The stroke changed her life dramatically, but she refuses to give up hope. "I will consider myself rehabilitated when I can be gainfully employed once again in my profession of nursing and have thereby reclaimed my life,"[9] she says.

Debra's story emphasizes that the effects of strokes can be long lasting. In many cases, they are permanent. Stroke is an impartial disease that can attack anyone, no matter how fit and healthy he or she appears to be.

No One Is Safe

The customary conception of stroke is that it is limited to the elderly, but recent statistics indicate that the average age of stroke victims is going down. Public-health officials attribute this to increased obesity among younger people and the rise in health problems that being overweight brings in its wake—high blood pressure, diabetes, and heart disease. The lifestyle factors that increase the likelihood of stroke include a diet that is high in fatty foods, lack of exercise, drug use, and participating in dangerous activities that are apt to lead to head injuries. Skateboarding or riding a bicycle without a helmet are two examples of this last risk factor.

Even fitness is no guarantee. Patrick Carey was a muscular member of the swim team at John Carroll University in Cleveland, Ohio, when he suffered a hemorrhagic stroke at the age of twenty-one. "I remember swimming that morning and I remember sitting in my dorm room doing my computer science homework," he says. "Next, I remember waking up in the intensive care unit."[10] Carey's right side was partially paralyzed, and his ability to speak was badly impaired. His stroke began when he sustained a tiny tear in his carotid artery, called a dissection, possibly caused by a cough. Dissection of an artery is the leading cause of stroke among teenagers and younger adults; hardening of the arteries is the principal reason the disease strikes older people.

"Any kind of sports, chiropractic manipulation, house painting, a sneeze, a cough—just turning your head quickly can lead to a dissection," says Dr. Dewitte Cross, director of Interventional Neuroradiology at Washington University's Barnes Jewish Hospital in St. Louis, Missouri. "It's hard to avoid all the things that might place you at risk."[11]

CHAPTER TWO

Symptoms and Diagnosis

Surviving a stroke and recovering from the damage it has caused depends almost entirely on how quickly the disease is diagnosed and treatment is administered. Brain tissue is extremely delicate and begins to die rapidly if it is deprived of blood. It is only recently, however, that doctors have begun to stress the need for immediate medical intervention in the case of stroke. "The importance of identifying stroke as a medical emergency has been underrated in the past, partly because it was assumed that not much could be done for stroke patients," says Dr. Vladimir Hachinski. "Today, the picture is changing. There is increased awareness of the dangers of stroke, and of the possibility of reducing the damage by taking quick, effective action."[12]

Before doctors can do their work, however, the stroke victim has a crucial role to play: He or she must recognize the symptoms of the onset of a stroke and take the appropriate action. This is not always easy. A stroke often comes on very suddenly, leaving little time for the victim to react before he or she becomes paralyzed or unconscious.

Edwin Jelks's stroke started with a feeling of heaviness in his left hand. The eighty-three-year-old military veteran ignored the symptom. "I possibly made my biggest mistake that morning," he says of the day in 1995 when a stroke changed his life forever. "I felt fine, but I laughingly told my wife that my left hand felt heavy. A heavy hand? How funny! (How uninformed can you be?) I had no pain and I was completely mobile . . . and I felt well except for that crazy left hand."[13]

Four hours later, Jelks was in a hospital emergency room. "I realized I could not turn over in bed," he says. "Then I found my whole left arm did not work. And my hand and my fingers would not work. My whole left side was paralyzed. I was afraid to check further."[14]

A stroke victim is likely to become aware of physical symptoms first, because these are often dramatic as well as sudden. They usually involve the loss of an ability the person has taken for granted during the course of his or her life.

Physical Symptoms of Stroke

A symptom of any disease develops when a person becomes aware of changes in his or her normal body functions. In the case of stroke, the most commonly reported sign of the onset of an attack is weakness, a symptom that can be interpreted in many ways, even by medical professionals. Many people assume that stroke induces paralysis, so they misjudge the situation when mere weakness is all they feel. Weakness caused by stroke usually affects more than one area on the same side of the body. Commonly linked areas of weakness occur in the face, arm, and hand; arm and leg; and face, arm, and leg. If the stroke is taking place in the brain stem, both sides of the body and all four limbs can be affected simultaneously.

Numbness is another frequent symptom of stroke. Patients describe the phenomenon either as a total loss of feeling in the affected body part or as a prickling, tingling sensation. "Some patients describe the feeling as if a line was drawn right down the center of their body with everything on one side of the line becoming numb,"[15] says Dr. Louis Caplan, a professor of neurology at Harvard Medical School, who has treated many stroke victims at Beth Israel Deaconess Medical Center in Boston, Massachusetts.

Loss of vision, usually in one eye, is another sign of stroke. This is usually symptomatic of a narrowing of the carotid artery and is often described by victims as a shade coming

Symptoms of Stroke

Sudden numbness or weakness of the face, arm, or leg, especially on one side of the body

Sudden trouble walking, dizziness, loss of balance or coordination

Sudden confusion, trouble speaking or understanding

Sudden trouble seeing in one or both eyes

Sudden, severe headache with no known cause

Source: American Stroke Association.

down from the top of the eye that eventually results in total, temporary blindness in that eye. A related symptom occurs when objects on one side of the patient's field of vision suddenly become invisible. The person becomes aware that something is wrong only when he or she bumps into one of those objects. Stroke-related blindness can last from a few seconds to several days or even months. Sometimes, it is permanent.

The fourth physical symptom of stroke is dizziness or loss of balance and coordination. All of these motor difficulties are likely to be accompanied by mental impairments. The mental symptoms of stroke are sometimes difficult for the victim to recognize because these aspects of the disease affect the ability to reason and draw conclusions from experience.

Mental Symptoms of Stroke

The brain is involved in speaking, thinking, remembering, regulating behavior, and interpreting visual space. A failure in any

Misdiagnosis Is All Too Common

Emergency room doctors are rarely specialists in stroke, and very often patients are misdiagnosed and sent home without getting the treatment they desperately need. Marissa Dusch was twenty years old when she woke up one morning with a sharp pain in her head. She also felt nauseated. The pain grew worse, and at 5:00 A.M. she walked into an emergency room.

At the hospital they gave me an anti-nauseant [a drug to ease upset stomach], told me it was probably flu and sent me home. I went home and lay down on the couch. At this point, it was about 8 am and I was feeling dizzy. I remember getting up off the couch, and then falling to the ground. I think I hit my head, but I can't remember.

So there I was, on the floor. My left side felt weird. It was so scary. It felt completely numb, like I didn't have a left side to my body. I yelled for help. My dad came and took me to the hospital. I was rushed to intensive care and given a whole bunch of tests.

I was drifting in and out of consciousness. They told my Dad, "She's had a stroke. She might not make it."

Dusch was transferred to a hospital better equipped to deal with stroke patients and made a full recovery.

Marissa Dusch, "In My Own Words," Heart and Stroke Foundation of Canada. ww2.heart andstroke.ca.

of these functions can be symptomatic of stroke. Two types of speech difficulties are often seen in stroke patients. They are called dysarthria and aphasia. Dysarthria is difficulty pronouncing words, and it is caused by a weakening of the muscles used in talking. Patients with this problem often have a lot of trouble communicating their symptoms to doctors, and this can delay appropriate treatment. However, these patients can understand words spoken to them, and they can write clearly. Aphasia refers to a condition in which the affected person uses wrong words or incorrect grammar when he or she speaks. Sometimes, the victims are unable to speak entirely, and they are often unable to understand the speech and writing of others who are trying to communicate with them. Again, this condition makes patient-doctor communication problematic.

In addition, people who have had strokes often have a great deal of difficulty remembering simple things, like recent events and conversations. They tend to repeat themselves and fail to remember that they have answered questions just minutes before. This short span of concentration is extremely frustrating to the patient. Stroke victims may also lose their sense of

Sudden difficulty in speaking, thinking, or remembering can be symptomatic of stroke.

space and proportion. People with this disability cannot draw the simplest shapes and will get lost in areas with which they are familiar, including their own homes. This confusion and disorientation sometimes leads to apathy: The victim loses interest in—or becomes afraid of—moving from one room to another, for example. In contrast, some sufferers respond by becoming hyperactive. They jabber endlessly, moving randomly from one topic to another, and exhibit nervous or jittery behavior.

Emotional and behavioral changes are also fairly common. Anger, anxiety, and frustration are frequently seen in people who have had a stroke but cannot understand what has happened to them or why other people are treating them differently from before. Frequent and dramatic swings of emotion sometimes afflict stroke victims as they grapple with the suddenly changed circumstances. Many become deeply depressed and withdrawn. These emotional reactions to stroke are difficult not only for those who experience them directly but also for those who are trying to help them.

In almost every case, a stroke is diagnosed by an emergency room doctor after the patient has been brought to the hospital. The symptoms are usually so dramatic that the victim or a witness to the attack calls for emergency help rather than waiting for a doctor's appointment. Most callers to doctors' offices in cases of stroke are immediately told to hang up and dial 911 to summon paramedics.

Preliminary Tests

Emergency room doctors are faced with a number of challenges when dealing with a patient suspected of having had a stroke. The first is determining whether or not a stroke did, in fact, occur. The second is discovering the type and cause of the stroke. The third is taking appropriate action to save the patient's life and limit the amount of brain damage sustained. The decisions are crucial. Misdiagnosing a hemorrhagic stroke for an ischemic stroke can prompt a doctor to initiate a course of treatment that could make the situation worse, not better. That happened, for example, when Israeli prime minister Ariel Sharon was given blood thinning agents following what was thought to be an ischemic stroke in 2006. The treatment caused massive bleeding in his brain and sent him into a lasting coma.

The first thing the emergency room staff does when dealing with a stroke patient is try to get an accurate description of the symptoms. Obviously, the best source of information is the patient, but if he or she cannot communicate, a family member or friend may be asked to answer the questions. This is the most important aspect of the assessment, because it often determines which course of action the doctors will take. Once the symptoms, both those that occurred during and immediately preceding the attack, and long-term changes in the patient's well-being have been ascertained, the staff will try to get a detailed medical history. This will include discerning other medical problems, medications being taken, the patient's general state of mind, and as much information as can be provided about the medical history of immediate family members. Stroke, like many medical conditions, has a genetic component and tends to run in families. Information about family members helps doctors in their assessment of the present crisis by providing clues about potential inherited weaknesses and predispositions.

Physical Examination

After the staff has collected as much information as it can, a doctor will conduct a physical examination of the patient. He or she will test the pulse at the wrist to determine heart rate and detect any abnormalities of the heart rhythm. The heart will be listened to through a stethoscope to check for murmurs. These odd rhythms may indicate problems with heart valves, a frequent cause of embolisms. The doctor may also use the stethoscope to get a quick reading of the sounds the patient's blood vessels are making as blood flows through them. A particular sound, called a bruit after the French word for "noise," is a good indication that a vessel has become narrowed. The carotid arteries are the most significant location of bruits in stroke patients.

The doctor will also administer preliminary neurological tests, searching for abnormalities in how the brain is working.

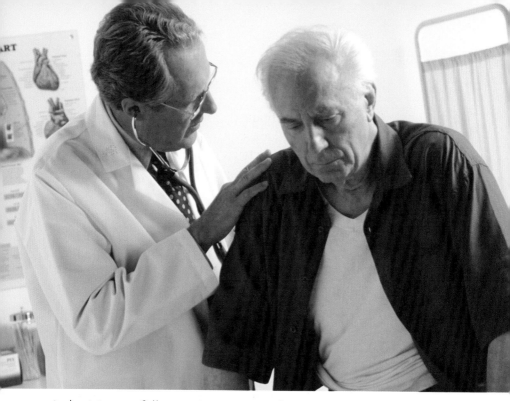

A physician carefully examines a patient for symptoms of stroke.

The physician will pay close attention to the patient's speech and ability to understand what is being said to him or her. The patient will be asked to repeat certain phrases and name objects in the examining room. The patient may also be asked to read a simple passage of written text and to write a brief paragraph on any subject that comes to mind. He or she may also be asked to look at pictures and describe what is going on in them or asked to draw simple objects to test whether the ability to deal with spatial relationships has been impaired. Memory tests will be given; the patient may be asked to name the current president of the United States, what day of the week it is, or to state his or her mother's maiden name.

In addition to this examination of mental function, the doctor will look into the patient's eyes and may administer an eye exam. He or she will test the strength of the patient's limbs and how the reflexes respond. Sensation will be tested by pricking the skin on the patient's arms and legs with a pin. In addition to these hands-on tests, doctors will take advantage of medical technology to confirm the diagnosis.

Brain Scans

Based on the information obtained from the physical examination, the doctor will then order a series of laboratory tests to evaluate the patient further. These tests will tell the doctor quickly and surely both if the patient has had a stroke and, if so, whether it was an ischemic or hemorrhagic stroke. They will also reveal what parts of the brain have been damaged and measure the extent of the destruction of brain cells. They will indicate the location and severity of arterial blockages and if the root cause of the attack was due to heart or blood abnormalities.

The first series of these tests will provide the doctor with images of the brain to make sure that abnormalities detected in the preliminary examination are due to stroke and not some other cause, such as a brain tumor. There are two methods to do this: computerized tomography (CT) and magnetic resonance imaging (MRI). In a CT scan, ordinary X-rays and computers are used to make images of thin slices of the brain, each slice providing a picture of the structures of part of the brain. MRI scans, on the other hand, use radio frequencies to displace water molecules slightly in the brain after they have been aligned in a strong magnetic field. As the molecules return to their original position, they emit magnetic energy that is captured in a visual image. An MRI can also make images of blood vessels in the brain. Says Dr. Caplan:

> Doctors sometimes order an intravenous injection of a substance that adds contrast to the images in order to show more detail. In CT this is usually an iodine-containing substance. Gadolinium is the chemical used for contrast in enhancement during MRI. Occasionally, patients have an allergic response to these contrast substances, especially to the dye used for CT contrast.[16]

Both CTs and MRIs show doctors whether there is bleeding in the brain or if the damage has been caused by a blocked artery. Bleeding shows up white on the scans; damage due to lack of blood caused by a blocked artery shows up black. Thus, a quick inspection of either one of these scans will tell the doctor whether the patient has suffered an ischemic or hemorrhagic

Undergoing Brain Scans

Being rushed to the emergency room in the midst of a suspected stroke can be a terrifying experience. A forty-two-year-old schoolteacher, who has chosen not to reveal her name but has created a Web site to help other stroke victims, talks about undergoing a CT scan and an MRI. Astonishingly, she has managed to keep her sense of humor:

> A CT scan is often called a "cat" scan, although I defy anyone to put a cat on a backboard, tell them to be perfectly still for five or so minutes while they put their head in what amounts to a giant donut, to be X-rayed. Try not to cough or sneeze 'cause it'll make you move and they'll have to start over!
>
> MRI technically means magnetic resonance imaging. Nice name, but what they actually do is make sure you are not wearing anything metal ('cause the magnet is pretty strong) and they strap you to a backboard. Like the CT scan, you aren't supposed to move. They roll you into a big round tube (kind of like a people-sized straw) that doesn't have enough room inside to even scratch your nose.
>
> You hear something spinning around outside of the straw and you'd swear they were banging on it with metal pipes. All in all, not the most relaxing experience. The feeling of claustrophobia, however, is less if you close your eyes and try to relax. Yeah, right.
>
> Anonymous, "On Being a Stroke Survivor," Who Stole My Other Side? www.deedoe.us.

stroke, a vital piece of information in determining what course of treatment to follow.

The scans also indicate where the abnormality is located and how extensive it is. They show if there is swelling due to a buildup of blood or due to damaged brain cells. Knowing the location of the abnormality permits doctors to assess which blood vessels supply the area and check them for clots or ruptures. Occasionally, a brain scan will come back normal in a patient who has had an ischemic stroke. This can confuse doctors and delay diagnosis, but it also indicates that no permanent damage has been done to the brain—in other words, that the blockage that caused the stroke has corrected itself, at least temporarily.

Blood Vessel Tests

Once the doctors have an idea, based on the brain scans, of where the blocked or ruptured artery that caused the stroke is located, they can pinpoint the exact site of the problem using tests that create images of the blood vessels themselves. The

A CT scan of a patient shows a ruptured artery as the cause of stroke.

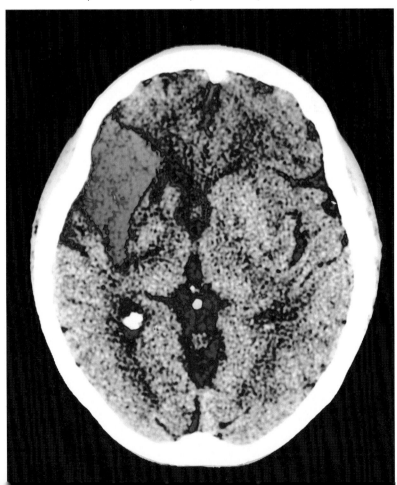

same CT scanner that took pictures of the brain can provide an image of an artery called an angiogram. An iodine dye is injected into a vein in the arm, then the CT scanner takes a rapid series of pictures charting the dye's flow through the veins and arteries in the rest of the body, including the brain. Similar images can be captured using an MRI machine. These pictures show exactly where the problematic artery is to be found and provide clues as to what should be done to correct the problem.

Doctors will also take advantage of ultrasound technology to measure the health of the patient's arteries. Ultrasound uses principles of sound waves to determine how well blood flows in the body. To assess blood flow in the arteries in and leading to the brain, probes are placed over the eyes, at the back of the neck, and over the temples, all places where the skull is nonexistent or at least thin enough to permit sound waves to be de-

An angiogram provides physicians with a detailed image of a patient's arteries.

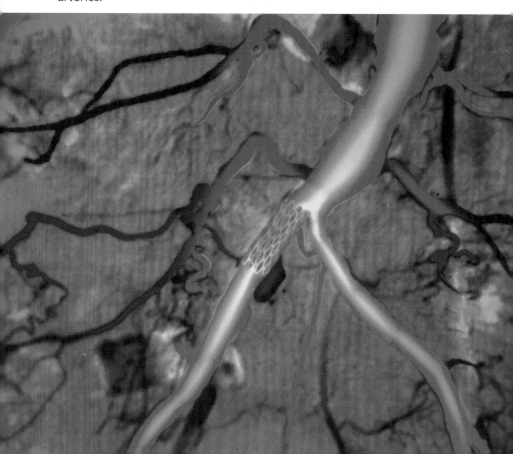

tected. If the artery is narrowed due to atherosclerosis or because of a clot that has partially obstructed it, the speed of the flowing blood will change at that point, and the ultrasound machine will be able to detect the change in sound.

Noninvasive Tests

There is another technique that can monitor how well blood is flowing through key arteries. Single photon emission computerized tomography (SPECT) can estimate the blood flow to a part of the brain. Dye containing a radioactive substance is injected, and the SPECT machine charts its flow through the brain's arteries. This will tell doctors which parts of the brain are receiving blood and which are not.

Tests of blood vessel health—CT scans, ultrasound, and SPECT—are all called noninvasive because, except for the injection of dye, the patient's body is not violated. If they fail to provide the information the doctor is seeking, the doctor may order an invasive test called a catheter angiogram. A catheter, a flexible tube with a tiny camera on one end, is inserted into one of the arteries of the arm or leg. A medical specialist, called a radiologist, manipulates the catheter through the maze of vessels into an artery in the neck. A dye is injected into the catheter, and a series of quickly taken X-rays follow its progress through the artery. The camera picks up any blockages or other abnormalities and displays them on a screen, where the radiologist can see them. The catheter test carries a small degree of risk in that it could dislodge a piece of plaque, a solid substance adhering to the wall of the artery, which could then create a blockage in a narrow artery in the brain.

Other Tests

At the discretion of the doctor in charge of the case, a stroke patient may be given other tests. Foremost among these are heart tests, because the heart is one of the most common sites of clot formation. An electrocardiogram (EKG) displays the rate at which the heart is beating and can pinpoint any irregularities in the rhythm of the beat. It can also reveal if the patient has had a heart attack in the past.

Ultrasound is also used to yield pictures of various parts of the heart and how they are working. The procedure is called echocardiography. An ultrasound probe is placed on the chest, and the patient swallows a string to which another probe is attached. The test examines the health of heart valves and the chambers of the heart as the organ beats.

Blood tests of various kinds are also routinely performed on stroke patients to discover the chemical composition of their blood and detect abnormalities that could have caused clots or bleeding. Lipid and cholesterol tests can reveal a propensity to hardening of the arteries and inflammatory conditions that sometimes contribute to strokes.

All these tests must be performed quickly after the patient is admitted to the emergency room. Some stroke treatments are useless if they are not administered within three hours of the attack, so physicians must be able to assess the patient's condition quickly and accurately if they are to provide the needed help.

CHAPTER THREE

Treatment

Treatment for stroke takes two forms: emergency treatment and long-term therapy. To be effective, emergency treatment must be initiated quickly. The need to recognize the symptoms of stroke and get medical help in a timely way is illustrated by the frontline emergency room treatment for ischemic stroke. Tissue plasminogen activator (tPA) is a clot-dissolving drug approved for use by the federal Food and Drug Administration in 1996 for use in the emergency care of stroke victims. Physicians have hailed tPA as a wonder drug, but it works only if it is administered to the patient within three hours of the onset of an ischemic stroke. "This makes it very important for people who think they are having a stroke to seek help immediately," says the American Stroke Association. "If given promptly, tPA can significantly reduce the effects of stroke and reduce permanent disability."[17]

When a stroke patient arrives at the emergency room, doctors are faced with a daunting deadline. They must complete a full evaluation in time to administer tPA while the treatment still has a chance to succeed. "It can take an hour or more to complete and interpret necessary tests like a CT scan, which have to be done before thrombolytic [tPA] therapy can be given,"[18] says Emily Shroeder, a researcher who studied the time it takes to deal with stroke patients in emergency rooms

How tPA Works to Reduce the Effects of Stroke

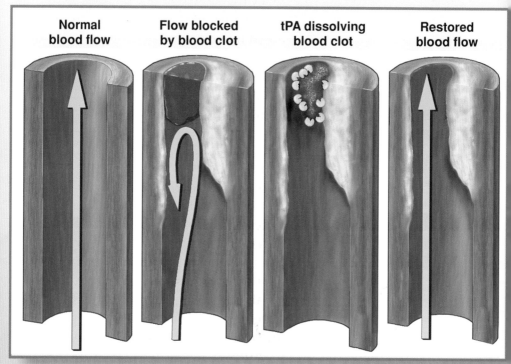

| Normal blood flow | Flow blocked by blood clot | tPA dissolving blood clot | Restored blood flow |

Tissue plasminogen activator (tPA) is a drug that dissolves the proteins that make up blood clots, thus reducing the effects of stroke. The drug must be administered to a patient within three hours of the onset of an ischemic stroke to be effective.

in three different American cities. Unfortunately, most patients do not arrive at the hospital until it is too late. "Currently, only about five percent of stroke patients arrive at the hospital in time to receive tPA because most people don't know the warning signs or don't realize they should seek medical help immediately,"[19] says Dr. Edgar Kenton, chair of the American Stroke Association Advisory Committee.

Dr. Vladimir Hachinski recounts two stories that forcefully illustrate the need for speed in treating stroke patients with tPA. In one case, a middle-aged woman was taken to an emergency room two hours after noticing the first symptoms of a stroke. Doctors gave her tPA, and within a month she had made a complete recovery. In the other case, a fifty-nine-year-old man got to the emergency room three hours after the onset of his attack. Doctors then evaluated him and administered tPA. "Hospital staff watched him closely for two hours, but their hope soon waned," Hachinski says. "He grew worse, and a CT scan of the brain showed that the drug had caused bleeding into the part of the brain deprived of blood and softened by swelling. All efforts to save him proved futile, and he died a few hours later."[20]

Emergency Treatments for Ischemic Stroke

Emergency treatment for ischemic stroke—the kind of stroke caused when a blood clot blocks an artery—takes three forms: unblocking the artery as quickly as possible to restore the flow of blood, the administration of drugs to prevent the formation of additional clots, and the use of medications to strengthen brain tissue to make it better able to resist damage.

Of these three strategies, the first is the most important, and it is the one that must happen quickly to minimize permanent damage to brain cells. Doctors prefer to use drugs like tPA to do this. There are about a dozen drugs approved for this use, but tPA is the most effective. The medication is delivered either by injection into a blood vessel in the arm or leg or, in extreme cases, through a catheter inserted directly into the blocked artery at the location of the clot. The drugs dissolve the clot and permit normal blood flow to resume. The injection can be dangerous if the patient's blood pressure is too high, if he or she is taking blood-thinning medicines, or if the patient has a condition that creates a propensity for internal bleeding.

If drugs fail to dissolve the clot, doctors can perform angioplasty, in which a probe is inserted into the blocked artery and the clot is broken up mechanically. As a last resort, a surgeon can operate and remove the clot. Sometimes, if removing the clot is deemed too risky, a procedure is done to bypass the blocked artery by severing it above and below the clot and then reconnecting it using a small piece of artery taken from elsewhere in the patient's body.

The next step is to administer anticoagulant or antiplatelet drugs to prevent new clots from forming. Platelets are substances in the blood that clump together to prevent bleeding; they form the mass of blood clots. Doctors must exercise extreme caution, because giving these medications to someone who has had a hemorrhagic stroke could worsen the bleeding and kill the patient. Sometimes, this step is accomplished by giving the patient nothing more complicated than aspirin, a very effective and inexpensive antiplatelet drug. If aspirin is not effective, there are a wide range of stronger drugs available for doctors to use.

Finally, doctors will give the patient neuroprotective drugs, medications that protect brain tissue from damage due to de-

Some stroke victims require surgery to remove blood clots or repair ruptured arteries.

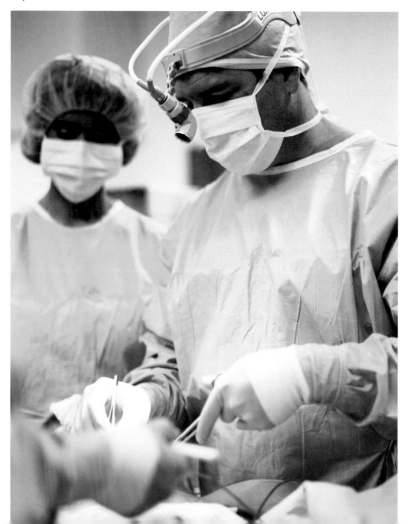

creased blood flow and help brain cells that have been deprived of blood resume their normal function. Neuroprotection is a relatively new strategy in emergency stroke treatment, and a number of drugs are being studied to determine effectiveness and safety. Another new technique is to lower the temperature of the brain so that it needs less energy to function while it tries to repair itself.

Emergency Treatments for Hemorrhagic Stroke

Dealing with hemorrhagic stroke requires a different approach and usually requires the skill of a brain surgeon. Unfortunately, qualified surgeons are not available at many small hospitals, and the patient must be transported to larger, better-staffed medical centers.

Although surgically entering the brain to stop bleeding is a very dangerous procedure, treatment of hemorrhagic stroke is less complicated than treating ischemic stroke because there are fewer options for the doctors to consider. "Treatment of bleeding inside of the head is more simple and direct than the complicated and multifaceted treatment of different aspects of brain ischemia,"[21] says Dr. Louis Caplan.

A surgeon can open the skull of the patient and suture the bleeding artery. Both ruptures and malformations of the arteries can often be solved by inserting catheters through which patches can be delivered to the site of the bleeding. In some cases, this can be accomplished without surgery by directing a focused beam of radiation at the damaged area. Brain hemorrhages can be drained to relieve pressure, and drugs to promote clotting—the reverse of what is done in cases of ischemic stroke—can be administered.

However, as in the case of ischemic stroke, speed is crucial. The longer brain cells are deprived of blood, the less likely they are to recover. One factor that complicates the emergency treatment of hemorrhagic stroke is the limited availability of neurosurgeons. If a hospital is not equipped specifically to deal with strokes, emergency room doctors might not be able to locate a neurosurgeon in time for him or her to get to the operating room and save the patient. This is a particularly serious problem in rural hospitals, although smaller urban hospitals also experience this difficulty.

In all cases of stroke, doctors attempt to do other things to stabilize the patient, such as getting blood pressure into normal range, reducing elevated temperature, and regulating the body's production of glucose. All these factors can affect the outcome of stroke treatment, and all of them must be taken into consideration by emergency room personnel, who must act quickly.

Even if emergency treatment is successful in saving the patient's life, the battle is not over. A number of serious complications can arise in the hours and days following stroke treatment, and many of them can be fatal if not dealt with quickly and appropriately. Both ischemia and edema, the swelling following a hemorrhagic stroke, can continue and must be monitored carefully. As the brain fights to repair the damage it has endured, the patient might experience seizures that must be controlled with medication. Since the patient is likely to be bedridden during the days following a stroke, conditions that afflict bedridden people are likely to arise. These include pneumonia, urinary tract infections, muscle spasms, bed sores, and depression.

Dr. Caplan explains:

> Some [patients] become angry at what they feel is unfair "punishment." They ask, "Why did God do this to me?" Others, who had ignored their own risk factors, feel guilty. . . . Many feel guilty at placing a burden on their spouses and other caregivers. Some stroke patients become depressed and hopeless about the future. One of the most important and yet most frequently overlooked complications of stroke is depression.[22]

Because of this, psychiatric intervention is often required, even in the early stages of treatment, before the patient has become medically stable. Doctors have come to realize that surviving a stroke depends not only on their skills, but also on the patient's attitude in the first stages of recovery.

Curing and Healing

Psychologist Caroline Bliss Isberg of the Cabrillo College Stroke Center in Aptos, California, draws a distinction between curing and healing in recovering from a stroke. "Curing is the province of the physician," she says. "Healing is something a physician can't do for a patient. Healing can only come from within the human individual. Healing is the physical, mental, emotional, social and spiritual process of becoming whole again."

Isberg identifies the stages of healing. First comes agonizing, characterized by shock, fear, and a sense of irreparable loss. The second stage is fantasizing, when the patient dreams that the condition will suddenly and miraculously cure itself. This quickly gives way to realizing that the impairments will require arduous therapy and may never disappear entirely. Anger and depression frequently accompany this stage.

The fourth stage is blending, in which the patient blends what life was like before the stroke with his or her present reality. That is followed by framing—finding new and positive meaning in the stroke experience. "Joy reenters life and leads the way toward the final stage—'owning'—characterized by determination, control and self-help," Isberg says.

Caroline Bliss Isberg, "An Exploration of Outcomes and Quality of Life Factors in an Educationally Based Rehabilitation Program," Cabrillo College Stroke Center. www.strokecenter.com.

The Treatment Team

Strokes can cause extensive damage to the brain. The organ, assisted by drugs, will fight hard to restore itself. Undamaged blood vessels will take over the jobs of those that have been damaged beyond repair by the stroke. If the clot or the bleeding was dealt with in time, the brain may be able to compensate for those cells that died, and the patient may be able to return to normal or close to normal. However, most stroke survivors need a lengthy period of in-hospital care before they can

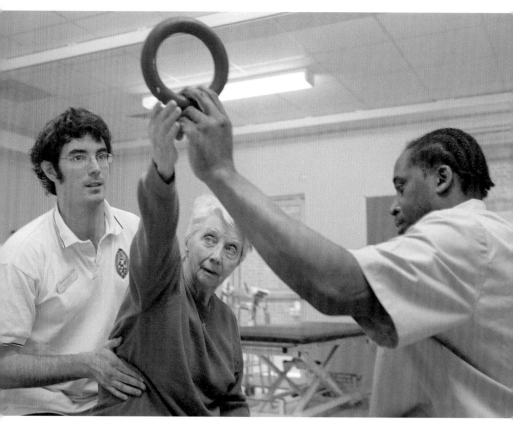

A positive attitude during physical therapy may help stroke victims like this woman heal psychologically.

return home. The early stages of stroke recovery require constant monitoring by a team of highly trained specialists.

At this stage, the patient is disoriented, and his or her physical condition can change rapidly and dramatically. "One of the most frightening aspects of a stroke is not knowing how it will affect you," says Dr. Vladimir Hachinski. "The extent of mental and physical disability depends on the type of stroke experienced and where it has damaged the brain. Even subtle differences in behavior or the ability to perform tasks can be frustrating for the survivor and the caregivers."[23]

Dealing with the effects of stroke in the immediate aftermath of emergency intervention requires the participation of the victim, his or her family and friends, and a team of professional caregivers. The treatment team consists of the doctor, nurses, a speech and language therapist, a phyical therapist, an occupational therapist, a social worker, a registered dietician, and a psychological counselor. A key aspect of the team approach to stroke rehabilitation is that the members of the team communicate with each other to make sure no facet of the patient's care is being overlooked. "The stroke rehabilitation team is a group of specialists and allied health professionals who work together to provide stroke survivors with the comprehensive medical care, therapy, counseling, and family training needed to recover from a stroke,"[24] says the Cleveland Clinic Foundation, an organization devoted to keeping the public informed on health issues.

Rehabilitation takes place both at inpatient facilities and on an outpatient basis once the patient is well enough to return home. At every step of the way, the survivor's physical, mental,

A speech therapist helps a man in whom the muscles used for talking have been weakened by stroke.

and emotional health must be monitored carefully. Each of these three aspects plays an important role in recovery.

The Task of the Rehabilitation Team

Rehabilitation begins as soon as the patient's life is no longer in danger. The immediate concern is to prevent a second stroke and avoid complications that could delay recovery. This aspect of care starts while the patient is still in the hospital. In some cases, the procedures are severe. For example, if the patient has difficulty swallowing, the treatment team may have to insert a feeding tube either through the nose or directly into the stomach. Proper nutrition is a key element of recovery from any illness. The patient may also need a urinary catheter to empty his or her bladder.

The Long Road to Recovery

Bob Nichols was a thirty-year-old broadcast journalist and avid golfer when he was felled by a stroke. He learned that the road to recovery involves hard work. The stroke paralyzed his left side and robbed him of his ability to speak. The two activities he loved most in life—golf and his broadcasting career—were both out of reach. "I just thought my life is over," he says.

Nichols's will to fight back returned when his doctor pessimistically told him he would never play golf or work again. "Everybody has a button that somebody can push," he says. "He really pushed my button."

Nichols dedicated himself to an extensive and exhausting program of rehabilitation and made a full recovery. "It took me a long time," he says. "Almost two years of constant therapy. My therapy was 12 hours a day, six to seven days a week. I decided I could do it, and I went about the cause of doing it. It was my 'job' for over two years."

Bob Nichols, "Stroke Survivors: Their Stories." www.poststrokehelp.com.

Even at this early stage in the patient's recovery, the physical therapist will perform range-of-motion exercises by moving the patient's limbs, fingers, and toes to counter any paralysis. Gentle movement of paralyzed limbs helps to decrease pain, keep joints and muscles flexible, and minimize bone loss due to inactivity. The speech therapist will also begin work as soon as possible to ensure that the muscles used in talking do not become weak.

Relapses are common in the early stages of stroke recovery, and the patient must be helped to overcome setbacks, which can be extremely disheartening and delay further progress. Dr. Vladimir Hachinski tells the story of a woman who had made some progress but relapsed as the gains came too slowly. She became depressed and apathetic, and her husband was powerless to help her. "She would melt into tears and complain that her life was over,"[25] Hachinski says. Eventually, her doctor recognized the symptoms of depression and intensified her inpatient psychological counseling, and her progress resumed.

The patient, the patient's family, and the treatment team have a monumental task to perform. The goal of rehabilitation is to enable the stroke survivor to reach the highest level of recovery possible and to become independent enough to return home and resume a normal life. If full independence is not a realistic goal, rehabilitation strives to make the person as independent as possible and help him or her adjust to the lasting consequences of the stroke.

CHAPTER FOUR

Long-Term Care

Recovering from a stroke, especially if it is a severe one, is a long and arduous process. Many victims never fully regain their normal functions. The National Stroke Association estimates that "10 percent of stroke survivors recover almost completely; 25 percent recover with minor impairments; 40 percent experience moderate to severe impairments requiring special care; 10 percent require care in a nursing home or other long-term care facility; 15 percent die shortly after the stroke."[26]

In general, recovery is most rapid at the beginning of the rehabilitation program, when the patient is encouraged by early positive results. Then, a long period of slow progress follows. The slow gains test the emotional strength of the patient, the family, and the caregivers. It is during this time that the patient must be monitored most closely for signs of depression. A patient must adjust to the reality that it can take years of sustained effort to regain the ability to do tasks that were once second nature.

Rehabilitation Outside the Hospital Setting

Once the patient's health has stabilized and there are no longer concerns of a second stroke or death, he or she is discharged from the hospital and sent to a rehabilitation facility that specializes in the care of stroke victims. Sometimes, the patient insists on going home directly. The rehabilitation team conducts a thorough evaluation before agreeing to this. Factors they take into consideration include lingering neurological abnormalities (the physical health of the brain as revealed by CT scans and MRIs among other criteria), medical problems relating to or independent of the stroke, difficulty walking and moving limbs, problems with speaking and understanding speech, mental alertness, and the ability to reason properly. The team also assesses whether the home is equipped to deal with someone at the patient's level of recovery (for example, is the bathroom on the second floor if the patient cannot climb stairs)

Stroke survivors who participate in physical rehabilitation programs adapt more easily to their altered lives after a stroke.

and how well prepared the family is to provide the needed care and support.

In most cases, the patient is strongly encouraged to spend time in a rehabilitation facility before making the transition to home. There are a number of options available. People whose health is fragile can choose to go into a facility that is staffed with doctors and nurses to provide around-the-clock medical surveillance and care. Those in better health may opt for a facility that provides intensive speech and physical therapy—three or more hours a day. These facilities are not equipped to deal with acute medical crises, but they provide a sustained level of therapy that most doctors feel is necessary if a stroke survivor is to reach full potential. There are also facilities that offer lower-intensity therapy for those patients whose impairment is not severe. Unfortunately, the decision on which facility is most suitable is often limited by the patient's ability to pay.

Finally, therapy can be continued on an outpatient basis if the patient can travel to the facility or in the home if he or she cannot. In keeping the patient active in rehabilitation, the participation of family and friends becomes crucial. "For rehabilitation to be successful, it is important for the patient and his or her family to cooperate and show enthusiasm," says the Patient Education Institute. "Even though rehabilitation has gotten much better in the last 20 to 30 years, stroke victims are still sometimes not able to get back to the way they were before the stroke. It is important to keep working on skills and not get discouraged."[27]

The challenges facing a recovering stroke patient frequently include full or partial paralysis, difficulty speaking, inability to deal with spatial relationships between objects, problems with memory and other mental functions, and emotional distress.

Paralysis

Stroke victims have a wide range of problems to deal with in their attempt to recover and reclaim their lives. Frequently, they experience partial paralysis of one or more limbs after an attack because the part of the brain that governed the use of those limbs has been damaged. "The paralysis may affect only

After a stroke, even simple tasks, such as putting together a puzzle, can require much effort and patience.

the face, an arm, or a leg or may affect one entire side of the body and face," says Dr. George Jacob. "This one-side paralysis is called hemiplegia. A related disability that is not as debilitating as paralysis is one-sided weakness or hemiparesis."[28] Though the affected limb has not been harmed, the mechanism that controls its function has been impaired. The mechanism whereby the brain sends messages through the central nervous system telling that limb what to do is not functioning properly and must be retrained. In a sense, stroke victims have to learn to use the affected limb all over again.

A physiotherapist encourages a young stroke victim in her rehabilitation efforts.

Paralysis creates problems with everyday activities like walking, dressing, eating, and using the bathroom. A stroke victim may find it hard to sit upright in a chair due to weakness. Eventually the muscles of the paralyzed region will lose mass and become even weaker if they are not exercised regularly. The longer a stroke victim remains paralyzed, the more difficult it becomes to recover from the condition, so physical therapists try to begin working with the affected body parts as soon as possible.

Therapy usually starts with the therapist doing all the work, bending and stretching the limb to keep it flexible, and allowing the patient to learn what it feels like when the limb moves.

At first the movements are small. Gradually, the therapist extends the limb through a greater and greater range of motion. If the therapy is successful, the patient's brain will become reprogrammed through the repetitive movement of the limb, and he or she will gradually become able to move the arm, leg, hand, or foot without the assistance of the therapist. About 85 percent of stroke survivors who start out unable to walk regain the ability at least to some extent, but many of them require walkers, wheelchairs, or scooters if they have to travel more than a few yards on foot. Recovery of arm and hand movement is more difficult than regaining use of the legs. Fine hand movements, those involved in grasping objects, are especially difficult to recover. Many right-handed survivors have to learn, with the help of their physical therapists, to write and do other things with their left hand.

Speech Problems

Approximately 40 percent of people who survive a stroke emerge with speech problems of one sort or another. Speech is affected when the stroke has damaged the left side of the brain. These speech difficulties are not evidence of mental impairment. Few aspects of stroke are more frustrating to those dealing with a stroke patient than his or her inability to speak or understand the speech of others. The problem often interferes with treatment because the patient cannot easily make his or her needs and feelings known, nor can he or she sometimes understand and follow instructions provided by caregivers.

There are two broad classifications of speech difficulties. Aphasia is a disorder of language. In expressive aphasia, the victim cannot put thoughts into words. In receptive aphasia, also called Wernicke's aphasia, the person cannot understand spoken or written language. Expressive aphasics understand what is being said to them, but they cannot find the right words to respond. Receptive aphasics can speak fluently, but what they say often makes no sense because the part of the brain that equates words and meanings is not functioning properly.

Another type of speech defect found in stroke patients is called dysarthria. Unlike aphasia, victims of this disorder have no trouble understanding language or formulating thoughts in words, but when they do speak, what they say is often so slurred that hearers cannot make out what is said. Some people with dysarthria often have trouble controlling the volume of their voices. Others have problems controlling the behavior of speech muscles such as those of the neck, lips, face, tongue, and throat. In this case, the patient does not have difficulty with language at all; rather, it is simply a case of not being able to use the muscles necessary to utter articulate speech. For example, such a person would be able to write fluently, while someone with aphasia would not be able either to write or speak.

Speech therapy usually restores some the stroke victim's verbal abilities, but it is a long and tedious process of relearning to speak and recognize speech through repetition. Depending on the severity of impairment, a patient may re-

During speech therapy, a stroke victim with aphasia practices putting her thoughts into words.

Strokes in Children

Children have been largely ignored in the medical battle to conquer stroke. It is a common misperception that children cannot have strokes, yet one thousand infants and five thousand older children have strokes every year. Between 10 and 25 percent of these young victims die from the attack.

Says reporter Lauran Neergaard, who interviewed a number of experts on pediatric stroke:

> Specialists once thought most survivors eventually would recover because children's brains are more "plastic" than adults', that is, they're more likely to reroute themselves around damage. But research shows more than half such patients will have permanent motor or cognitive disabilities.
>
> There's little research on how to treat child stroke. Neurologists cobble together therapy based on what works in adults, although what causes most adult strokes—hardened, clogged arteries—isn't the culprit for youngsters, and few are diagnosed fast enough to try the drug tPA, which can restore their elders' blocked blood flow.

Lauran Neergaard, "Thousands of Kids Have Strokes: Doctors Look for Answers," *Seattle Times*, December 6, 2005. http://seattletimes.nwsource.com/html.

quire years of speech therapy without fully recovering. Penny Montgomery-West, whose businessman husband had a stroke at the age of forty-four, recalls their mutual frustration at the aphasia he suffered.

> My husband seemed to be trapped in his body without the ability to communicate. We both had to deal with fear, anger, depression, and isolation. Would he be able to participate as an active family member again, with the children, relatives, and friends? Would we, as a couple, ever be able to have an intimate relationship again? Would he ever be able to work again and support the family?[29]

Montgomery-West's husband had daily speech therapy for six months before his insurance ran out. Thereafter, he paid for twice-weekly sessions. He regained a small portion of his language skills, but he could not return to work, and they both saw their circle of friends dwindle as he struggled to overcome his disability. Eighteen months after suffering his stroke, Montgomery-West's husband had regained just enough of his ability to communicate verbally to go to work for the National Aphasia Association.

Paralysis and speech impairment are the most obvious effects of a stroke, but there are others that, while less apparent to an observer, cause the patient a great deal of anguish.

Sensory Problems

Pain is not usually associated with stroke, yet many stroke victims are in constant pain due to a sensory disorder called parathesia. The problem is little understood, and therapy has only limited success in alleviating it. Explains Dr. Louis Caplan:

> The body's sensory system can be simply thought of as having two different types of sensibilities. One type is related to coarse sensations, such as the perception of pain and temperature. Other sensations are fine and precise, and relate to touch. . . . The finer sensations predominate when all of the nerve pathways are intact. When these more precise sensory abilities are defective . . . then all stimuli seem to evoke only coarse unpleasant sensations that often are described as very hot, very cold, or stabbing.[30]

For parathesia sufferers, even slight pressure on an arm or leg can cause intense pain. Unlike normal pain, which is centered in the part of the body directly affected, the pain experienced by stroke victims seems to permeate their entire bodies. It is estimated that 50 percent of stroke victims experience this kind of pain to some degree and that 10 percent are severely affected by it. The only proven solution is pain-killing drugs, which are dangerous and often addictive. Some patients respond to electronic stimulation of the brain, but that treatment is controversial because it has not been extensively tested in stroke patients. Most people rely on therapy to help them learn to manage their pain psychologically.

Other sensory problems experienced by stroke survivors include loss of feeling in the limbs, chest, and abdomen along one side of the body. The effects can be insignificant, like not being able to tell the difference between a nickel and quarter held in the palm of the hand, or they may involve total loss of sensation. For example, the inability to feel heat often results in burns because the victim does not know to withdraw from the heat source. Some patients report alternating sensations of numbness or tingling and pain in various parts of their bodies, but this symptom is rare.

Sensory problems can also disturb vision. Some people report being unable to see objects on one side of their bodies, a continuation of one of the symptoms commonly suffered at the onset of a stroke. As in the case of pain, therapy is often not very effective in treating this type of disability. The patient must wait for the brain to figure out how to deal with sensory input in new ways, compensating for brain cells that were permanently damaged by the stroke. Only rarely does the victim fully recover these functions, and unfortunately this consequence of stroke must be endured.

Cognitive Problems

Another lingering effect of stroke is cognitive impairment. This injury strikes at the heart of the patient's sense of identity because it affects the ability to think, reason, and remember. Memory loss is one of the most frustrating problems faced by recovering stroke patients. Both sides of the brain are involved in cognition, but thoughts and recollections tend to be more concentrated on the left side. A stroke that damages the brain's left hemisphere can leave a patient with amnesia, the inability to remember events and the names of people and objects. Some victims are unable to remember conversations that took place in the very recent past. They ask the same questions over and over and repeat themselves incessantly.

The most frequent cognitive difficulty is anomia, the inability to remember names, and problems remembering spatial

Usually considered signs of aging, memory loss and confusion are also some frustrating effects of stroke.

directions are also fairly common. This latter impairment is especially frustrating when the locations involved were extremely familiar to the person before the stroke occurred. For example, some patients cannot remember how to get to the bathroom from the living room in their own homes. All these forms of memory loss can last for days, weeks, months, or even years after the stroke has occurred. Some memories may be lost forever.

Other forms of cognitive impairment affect a person's ability to plan activities. Many stroke survivors have a hard time putting events in proper sequence, making it difficult for them to make correct decisions concerning their daily lives. For example, stroke victims may not remember the proper sequence of steps involved in preparing a meal or getting dressed. The more complex the task, the more difficulty they have. Some get stuck on one activity in the sequence and repeat it over and over.

Cognitive therapy can usually help the stroke victim recover most of the lost cognitive ability, but, like other forms of therapy, it typically takes a long time. Customarily, the therapist will write down step-by-step instructions for the tasks the patient has to accomplish during the course of a typical day. Practicing doing each step in the proper order allows the patient to improve over time. As one type of cognitive ability returns, others tend to follow, because the brain slowly rewires itself as the therapy progresses. Therefore, learning how to make dinner, or any other task the patient used to perform on a regular basis, helps recover other lost memories. The therapist must encourage the stroke victim to be patient and accept that mental processes will be slower than they used to be.

Emotional and Behavioral Problems

In addition to cognitive impairments, emotions and behavior frequently change drastically when a person suffers a stroke. People who were once happy and optimistic may become sad and critical. Others who were even-tempered often become irritable.

Many stroke survivors lose the capacity to make emotional connections. They seem to lose interest in loved ones and in activities they used to enjoy. They cannot detect and evaluate the emotional state of others and often respond inappropriately. For example, a patient may not realize that his wife is angry or frustrated and may uncharacteristically make light of the stress she is under rather than reacting sympathetically. This is the source of a lot of the frustration that family members and caregivers feel when trying to help a stroke victim cope with his or her disabilities.

Conversely, other stroke survivors experience a kind of false euphoria, or feeling of well-being, that does not reflect their circumstances. They may laugh hysterically at situations normally thought to be tragic. Most of these people also have pronounced difficulty with muscle control, so their emotional outbursts can be dramatic and upsetting to those around them. Many patients who have this problem are aware that their reactions are inappropriate, but they cannot control them. Consequently, they often try to avoid contact with others.

Occasionally, people undergo radical personality changes. British stroke survivor Mark Tolley reports:

A Family Crisis

Families of stroke victims often suffer as much as the patient. "Stroke is a crisis that hits the entire family," speech pathologist Dr. Gail Gurland told reporter Georgia Dullea.

The tragedy takes many forms. Dullea writes:

> An aged couple is having a leisurely breakfast in a diner when, suddenly, the man explodes in a torrent of obscenities. Leaning across the table, his wife sings softly into his ear, "Happy birthday to you, happy birthday to you." The man falls silent.

> Another woman bends over a bed to straighten her husband's socks. It has taken an hour to bathe and dress him and she is exhausted. She has forgotten that he likes to have the cuffs of his socks turned in a certain way. Engraged, he lashes out with his working arm, striking her. She begins to sob.

There are no official statistics on divorce among couples in which one partner has suffered a stroke, but therapists say the incidence is high. Dullea reports: "In the weeks and months after a stroke, the patient may be irritable, demanding, self-centered. Unexplained bursts of crying or laughing are common. So are periods of depression, apathy and rage. While these symptoms generally disappear in time, they take their toll on the family."

Pat Singer, whose husband was recovering from a stroke, told Dullea: "You could break up your marriage very easily or put your mate away in a home very easily. You have to understand you're not married to the same guy. . . . My husband was a very macho man. He was the boss in our house. Now, I'm the boss, the mother, everything."

Georgia Dullea, "Relationships: Families as Victims of Stroke," *New York Times*, May 9, 1983. www.nytimes.com.

Even more than other illnesses, stroke places enormous stress on family relationships.

I changed from a loud mouth lad who would speak for the sake of speaking to an altogether quieter person—but I started to learn things and considered other peoples' points of view and I became very angry with others who wouldn't or couldn't do the same. . . . In other ways, it made me more extroverted. If we went to a nightclub, I would be the first on the dancefloor. . . . I traveled around the world on my own, and that was totally out of character.[31]

Stroke victims with cognitive disabilities do not have diminished intelligence. They score as high on IQ tests as they did before suffering their attacks. The nature of their disabilities lies in the failure of their brains to interpret external signals properly. Thus, stroke victims become extremely frustrated and resentful if the people they deal with treat them like children or as if they were intellectually challenged. They frequently require psychological counseling to help them deal with this type of frustration.

Recovering from a stroke is a long process that requires a lot of patience on the part of all involved, especially family and friends of the victim. To them, it often seems they are dealing with a different person and not the one they had known and loved.

CHAPTER FIVE

Prevention

Public-health officials estimate that about 85 percent of strokes could be prevented, even though half of all strokes occur in people who have no prior symptoms. That means that 50 percent of stroke victims have no warning that they are going to have an attack and no opportunity to take last-minute steps to prevent the attack from occurring. Prevention, therefore, depends on learning the risk factors of stroke and taking steps to minimize them. "Risk factors are traits and lifestyle habits that increase the risk of disease," says the American Stroke Association. "Extensive clinical and statistical studies have identified several factors that increase the risk of stroke. Many of them can be modified, treated or controlled. Some can't. The more risk factors you have, the higher your chances of having a stroke. The best way to prevent a stroke is to reduce your stroke risk factors."[32]

Making lifestyle changes to lower the likelihood of stroke is especially important for people who have one or more of the risk factors that cannot be controlled. One of the primary uncontrollable risk factors is age. Although people of all ages, even children, have strokes, the older a person is the greater his or her risk for stroke. Apart from age, there are other risk factors that are beyond control. For example, stroke is more common among men than women. However, women are more likely to die from a stroke. In fact, women, although they have fewer strokes than men, account for half of all stroke-related deaths. Woman who are pregnant or taking birth control pills are particularly susceptible.

Even genetics plays a role. The risk of stroke is greater if a parent, sibling, or grandparent has had a stroke. African Americans are more likely to have a fatal stroke than other groups, but researchers are not clear why this is so. To a lesser degree, Asians and Hispanics have a higher rate of stroke than the general population. Finally, among the risk factors that cannot be

Adopting a healthy lifestyle, including eating a well-balanced diet, can help reduce the risk of stroke.

directly controlled are incidents of previous strokes and heart disease. Someone who has had a stroke is far more likely to have another than someone who has never had a stroke at all. Those who have had heart attacks are similarly at greater risk for stroke than those who have not.

Transient Ischemic Attack

Although it is true that most strokes occur without prior warning, many are preceded by a definite danger signal that most people—and some doctors—ignore. A transient ischemic attack (TIA) has been called a ministroke, and it often precedes a major brain attack by days, weeks, or even months. Ten percent of people who experience a TIA have a major stroke within ninety days. Because the effects of a TIA are so short-lived—they pass in a matter of seconds—both patients and doctors used to regard it as a nonthreatening event. "Transient ischemic attack is no longer considered a benign [harmless] event but rather a critical harbinger [warning] of impending stroke," says Dr. Nina Solenski of the University of Virginia Health Sciences Center in Charlottesville, Virginia. "Failure to quickly recognize and evaluate this warning sign could mean missing an opportunity to prevent permanent disability or death."[33]

More than half a million TIAs are reported in America every year, and many more go unreported. The symptoms are like those of a stroke except they last for only a few seconds, after which the patient returns to normal. Because they pass quickly and leave no lasting impairment, they seem to be of little consequence. That is why most TIAs are overlooked by the person experiencing them. According to the American Stroke Association, if victims of TIAs took them seriously, approximately fifty thousand strokes could be prevented each year in America.

The most common symptoms of a TIA are blurred vision, weakness in one arm or leg, difficulty swallowing, loss of balance, slurring of words, confusion, temporary memory loss, and agitation. TIAs have the same cause as strokes—restricted blood flow to the brain caused either by partially blocked arteries or minor arterial bleeding. Left untreated, these underlying causes will only get worse and possibly lead to a full-blown

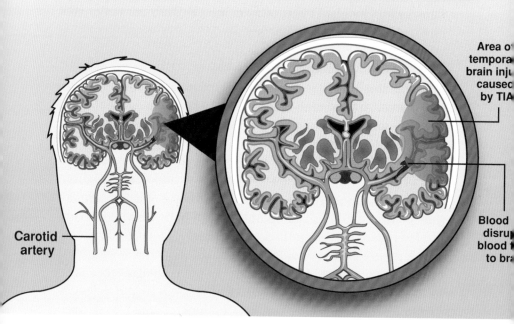

Transient Ischemic Attack

A transient ischemic attack (TIA) occurs when the blood supply to part of the brain is temporarily blocked by a blood clot. TIA symptoms are similar to those of stroke but usually last only a few seconds until the blood flow is restored.

Area o
tempora
brain inju
caused
by TIA

Carotid
artery

Blood
disru
blood
to bra

stroke. Solenski urges immediate action if anyone experiences even one of these signs. "Most patients with possible TIA should be sent to the nearest emergency department," she says. "To speed evaluation, it is appropriate to activate 9-1-1 Emergency Medical System for support."[34]

Taking a TIA seriously is one way to be proactive in preventing a major stroke. Stroke experts strongly urge people of all ages to take steps to deal with risk factors for the disease that are within their control. The foremost among these is high blood pressure.

High Blood Pressure

High blood pressure, also known as hypertension, is extremely common among adult Americans, and recently doctors have begun to notice an upsurge in this condition among younger people as well. The disease has a variety of physical and dietary causes, but the body's natural reaction to all of them is to thicken artery walls. If this did not happen, the extreme pressure the arteries are under would cause them to burst. However, this defense mechanism works only up to a point. Eventually, the blood vessels become brittle, increasing their tendency to close off or rupture. The delicate blood vessels of the brain are especially vulnerable. In addition, high blood pressure forces the heart to pump harder. Over time, this vital organ becomes enlarged and weak, raising the likelihood of blood clots.

Blood pressure can be controlled through diet, exercise, and medication. People with this condition should limit the amount of sodium in their diets. The principal source of sodium is salt, which is added to almost all processed foods. Care must be taken to ensure that too much salt is not consumed. There are a wide range of drugs available to treat high blood pressure,

Regular exercise lowers blood pressure and can prevent strokes.

and new ones are under development. However, like stroke itself, high blood pressure has few, if any, recognizable symptoms. It is believed that as many as half the people who suffer from hypertension are unaware of it. Luckily, blood pressure testing is easy and painless and is part of every routine medical examination.

Another important risk factor related to high blood pressure is heart disease. Heart valve disease can lead to stroke, because improperly functioning heart valves are one of the most frequent places where blood clots form. All types of heart disease diminish blood flow to the heart, often resulting in heart attack. During heart attacks, clots often form, and these are then ejected into the bloodstream and can ultimately cut off blood flow to the brain. The most common forms of heart disease are preventable by getting a sufficient amount of exercise and following a diet that is low in saturated fat, the type of fat found in animal products—meat, poultry, and dairy.

Contributing Factors

Another common medical condition among adults is high cholesterol, and this condition also makes people vulnerable to stroke. Cholesterol is a fatty substance produced by the liver, and it is therefore found in foods that come from animals. If there is too much cholesterol in the bloodstream, it tends to form hard deposits, called plaque, on the walls of the arteries that supply the brain and heart with blood. Cholesterol comes in two forms: Low-density lipoproteins (LDL) contribute to the formation of plaque, and high-density lipoproteins (HDL) help to block that process. Therefore, high LDL and low HDL counts are both potential warning signs of stroke. Again, a diet low in high-cholesterol foods and saturated fats, and plenty of exercise are the best ways to guard against cholesterol problems. Drugs are available to treat extreme cases, but many of these can damage the liver and thus are not prescribed often.

High blood pressure, heart disease, and elevated cholesterol levels are usually associated with obesity, a term that describes a condition in which people are seriously overweight. They can also be induced by diabetes. Both obesity and diabetes have been on the rise in America and other industrialized countries in recent years.

Obesity and Diabetes

For many years, doctors ignored obesity as a risk factor in stroke. While they encouraged their patients to maintain a proper weight for general health reasons, they overlooked it as a serious complication in people who had other indications that they were susceptible to stroke. However, a study conducted in Sweden in 2005 changed the medical perspective on obesity and stroke significantly.

The Swedish researchers studied more than seventy-four hundred men between the ages of forty-seven and fifty-five and found that strokes were 93 percent more frequent in men who were seriously overweight compared with those whose weight was considered to be normal or low. Another study done at the Harvard University Medical School discovered that women who gain a substantial amount of weight during their adult years double their risk of ischemic stroke. Too much body fat leads to high blood pressure, heart disease, hardening of the arteries, and high cholesterol levels. Extra weight, however, does not seem to play a role in hemorrhagic stroke. Still, stroke specialists now encourage their overweight patients to lose pounds as a routine method of reducing stroke risk.

Doctors have also noted an unusual frequency of strokes among people who suffer from diabetes. Diabetes is a disease in which the body cannot properly process glucose, a form of sugar, either because the pancreas does not produce enough insulin, a hormone that permits cells to utilize glucose for energy, or because cells are resistant to the insulin available to them. In either case, glucose builds up in the bloodstream, causing, among other things, the arteries to harden, setting the stage for stroke.

Moreover, people with diabetes who suffer a stroke tend to recover less well than nondiabetics. "There has been considerable debate about why this occurs," say Professors Peter Coleman and Stephen Davis of Royal Melbourne Hospital in Australia. "It could be that the increase in glucose . . . is

Obesity leads to high blood pressure, heart disease, elevated cholesterol, and diabetes, all of which can contribute to stroke.

directly toxic to nerve cells in the brain."[35] Diabetes can be controlled through diet and exercise. A number of oral medications are available to control glucose levels, and, if they don't work, injections of insulin can compensate for the body's failure to deal with blood sugar.

Doctors have detected a number of other controllable risk factors associated with strokes. While not as significant as those dealt with in the preceding paragraphs, experts advise patients to encourage their doctors to test for them and prescribe appropriate forms of treatment.

Other Risk Factors

Many other risk factors for stroke concern blood disorders. For example, anemia—a lack of iron in the blood—is a significant stroke risk factor, and it can easily be treated with dietary supplements. High and low platelet counts are also significant. A low count indicates a susceptibility to bleeding and hemorrhagic stroke; a high count makes the blood clot and could lead to ischemic stroke. Both conditions are controllable through medication.

Pregnancy also raises the risk of stroke. Pregnant women and women who take oral contraceptives have blood that tends to clot. In pregnancy, this prevents excessive bleeding in the uterus and is necessary to protect the health of the unborn baby, but it can also lead to unwanted clots and ischemic stroke. The hormones in birth control pills also promote blood clotting and should be taken in the lowest possible effective dose. The same holds true for hormone replacement therapy, which many women take advantage of to ease the symptoms of menopause. Again, the smallest effective dose is recommended.

People with certain medical conditions should be aware that these illnesses can make them candidates for stroke and take steps to minimize other risk factors. Although medical researchers have not been able to pinpoint physical causes, statistics show the illnesses most usually associated with increased stroke risk include cancer, AIDS, infections, and inflammatory diseases such as lupus, arthritis, ulcerative colitis, and Crohn's disease. These last two ailments are conditions of the intestinal tract.

Experts also warn that a number of medicines can increase stroke risk and should be used with caution. Many nasal sprays, available without prescription to treat the symptoms of cold, flu, and allergies, contain chemicals that mimic the effects of the hormone adrenaline and can cause strokes by raising blood pressure. The diet drug fen-phen was pulled off the

Strokes and Surgery

People who undergo any surgery are at increased risk of stroke in the hours and days following the operation and must take precautions to avoid a tragic outcome. The risk seems to be brought about by the drugs given to surgical patients to limit bleeding. Sometimes these medications promote the formation of clots, which then cause ischemic strokes. The phenomenon is not common, but it can have momentous consequences.

Garrett Keller was just fifteen months old when he underwent routine surgery to correct a congenital heart defect. While he was recovering from the operation, he suffered a massive stroke that destroyed one-quarter of his brain. Now six years old, Garrett has short-term memory loss, partial blindness in one eye, and weakness throughout the entire right side of his body. He suffers from anxiety and often picks at his skin until it bleeds. If he hears people laughing, he assumes they are making fun of him. He was kicked out of kindergarten three times because he could not control his behavior.

"He gets very, very angry and then very, very happy, like a puppy," says his mother, Kathy Keller. "We send our kids out to make their own way. I send Garrett out, but he doesn't have the same tools everyone else has. That's a constant sadness for me."

Quoted in Alexandra Fleming, "Devastating Reality of Brain Injury: Trauma Affects Families, Finances, and Emotions," *Washington Times*, 2003. www.birf.info.com.

market because it was found to contribute to heart attack and stroke because, like adrenaline, it raises blood pressure. Herbal supplements that contain ephedra or ma huang can also be harmful, though they are still widely available. A 2003 study published in the *Journal of the American Medical Association* says these supplements can triple the risk of certain stroke-causing heart-rhythm problems. Other drugs and herbal supplements that promote thinning of the blood may contribute to conditions necessary for hemorrhagic stroke. Aspirin and garlic, because they are both blood thinners, can increase the risk of bleeding in the brain.

Lifestyle

Many people have developed lifestyle habits that put them in danger of stroke. The worst of these habits is smoking. Says Dr. Vladimir Hachinski:

> Smoking is a proven risk factor for heart disease and stroke, both hemorrhagic and ischemic. It causes direct damage to the lining of the arteries by breaking down elastin, the fibrous protein that gives flexibility to the

Smoking is a proven risk factor for stroke, one that is entirely avoidable.

blood vessels. . . . Smoking is a particularly high risk for women. Statistically, men are heavier smokers than women, but women reportedly are more addicted to nicotine. The risk of a ruptured aneurism in a female heavy smoker (35 cigarettes a day or more) is 11 times that of a woman of the same age who does not smoke.[36]

Another common lifestyle choice, the excessive consumption of alcohol, is known to increase the incidence of both heart attack and stroke. "Alcohol . . . abuse should be among the possible causes considered in cases of stroke, especially in young adults," says Dr. P.B. Gorelick of the University of Chicago Pritzker School of Medicine. "As [it is] potentially remediable, primary care physicians may play an important role in the reduction of stroke by implementing educational and preventive measures among their patients."[37]

Alcohol's danger lies in the fact that it acts as a blood thinner. Even moderate alcohol consumption may heighten the likelihood of stroke. Studies conducted in the 1990s showed that one or two drinks a day reduced the risk of heart disease, but where strokes are concerned, the benefits were not definitive. The British Stroke Association reports:

> Nearly nine out of 10 strokes are ischemic—caused by blood clots blocking the arteries. As with heart attacks, small amounts of alcohol seem to help protect against this types of stroke. The remaining percentage of strokes are hemorrhagic—bleeding caused by burst blood vessels in or around the brain. Alcohol does not protect against hemorrhagic strokes and even relatively small amounts can double or treble the risk of having a hemorrhagic stroke. Recent research has also shown that heavy drinking increases the risk of all types of stroke.[38]

In addition to alcohol abuse, drug abuse is a major cause of stroke among otherwise healthy young people. "Cocaine can give rise to brain hemorrhages, and it increases blood pressure tremendously," says Hachinski. "This combination—weakened blood vessels and increased blood pressure—sets the stage for a stroke. Heroin use also increases the risk of stroke dramati-

Marijuana and Stroke

A study in the journal Pediatrics *shows that bingeing on marijuana does pose a danger. Pediatric neurologist Dr. Thomas Geller examined the cases of three teenage boys who smoked the drug only very occasionally but consumed large amounts of it when they did use it. All three teens suffered strokes, even though they were otherwise healthy. Geller says:*

> Although reported strokes associated with marijuana use are few, marijuana use may represent a genuine risk factor for stroke. Here were teenagers bingeing on marijuana, some of whom are inexperienced. It sounds like the typical way many teens use it.

The novice marijuana user may be at greater risk of stroke, especially if they use a lot at one time.

Thomas Geller, "Rare Risk: Adolescent Binging on Marijuana Linked to Stroke," St. Louis University Press Releases. www.slu.edu/readstory/more/4283.

Like smoking tobacco, marijuana use can cause stroke.

cally, by causing the blood vessels to become inflamed. Moreover, the use of dirty needles can cause a blood infection in the heart valves which can produce clots that go to the brain."[39]

Diet and Exercise

Most doctors agree that the best way to avoid stroke is to eat a healthy diet and get a moderate amount of exercise. The doctors at St. Luke's Episcopal Health Systems in Houston, Texas, state on their Web site, "Although diet is not a lone ranger in stroke prevention, it is a big player in the reduction of two major risk factors for stroke: high blood pressure and elevated lipid [fat] levels like cholesterol and triglycerides."[40] Just as a diet that is high in saturated fats can increase the risk of stroke, a low-fat diet can offer a significant level of protection.

Nutritional experts advise that fruits and vegetables should be the mainstay of a stroke prevention diet. "A number of large-scale studies have repeatedly shown that people who eat plenty of fruits and vegetables have a lower risk of stroke," says the British Stroke Association. "Fruits and vegetables are known to contain a number of valuable nutrients, including antioxidants, fiber and folic acid, which may be responsible for their protective effects."[41] Antioxidants protect the body's cells from damage from harmful molecules that have been linked to stroke. Folic acid, found in leafy green vegetables like spinach, reduces blood levels of a chemical called homocysteine, which has been connected to arterial damage.

Studies have also shown that a diet rich in whole grains—products made from unprocessed wheat and other sources of flour—can cut the occurrence of stroke almost in half. Vitamin E, found in nuts and vegetable oils, also plays a role in reducing stroke risk, as do the essential fatty acids that occur in fish like salmon, mackerel, and sardines. Embracing a healthy diet, then, can help ward off some of the risk factors associated with stroke.

Exercise also plays an essential role in stroke prevention, doctors say. "New scientific studies have found that being moderately to highly active during leisure time significantly reduces the risk of stroke later in life,"[42] writes journalist Angela

Families who exercise together help reduce one another's risk for stroke.

Williams, reporting on research into the relationship between exercise and stroke conducted in Finland. The Finnish study, which mirrors a large number of similar studies elsewhere, looked at the behavior of forty-seven thousand people between the ages of 25 and 64. It learned that stroke risk was 26 percent lower in highly active people and 14 percent lower in those who were moderately active. For the purposes of the study, high activity was defined as more than three hours a week of intense physical exercise such as running, swimming, or playing competitive sports. Moderate activity was defined as more than four hours a week of light walking or bicycling or light gardening. The National Stroke Association recommends thirty minutes of brisk walking a day as the minimum amount of exercise required to reduce stroke risk.

Stroke experts conclude that if people were to follow a healthy lifestyle and avoid the major risk factors for stroke, the incidence of the disease could be diminished. They suggest that patients should discuss their stroke risk with their doctors and take steps to minimize the danger of falling victim to this condition.

CHAPTER SIX

The Future

Most doctors are encouraged by the progress that is being made in stroke research. Until twenty-five years ago, stroke was regarded as one of the inevitable consequences of aging, and many physicians took the view that the absence of apparent symptoms left them powerless to deal with it. However, a new mood of optimism has taken root in the medical community. "The current outlook for stroke patients is better than ever before," says Dr. Vladimir Hachinski. "Education, research and information are developing rapidly, and creating a future that looks even brighter than the present."[43]

Dr. Louis Caplan concurs that doctors have now come to a greater understanding of the causes of strokes and that medical technology has improved both diagnostic and treatment procedures. "The understanding of stroke seems to have come of age," he says. "The United States government, the American Academy of Neurology, and the American Stroke Association have all pressed for more research and more availability of expert care for stroke patients. Clearly, there will continue to be important advances in knowledge about the various causes of stroke and treatment."[44]

Advances are occurring on three principal fronts: new diagnostic techniques, new drugs and therapies, and new emphasis on getting needed treatment to patients in time to do them some

Medical researchers, such as these women in a lab, have made great strides in understanding the causes and treatment of stroke.

good. All three aspects of the war against stroke have seen exciting progress, and the advances have encouraged a greater number of researchers to focus their attention on stroke.

Previously, stroke research lagged behind the scientific study of heart disease and cancer in terms of funding. That is still true, but the gap is narrowing due to pressure from medical and patient lobbying groups, which are compelling the government and privately owned business to move stroke higher on the research agenda. Surveys indicate the public is gradually becoming more aware of strokes and the causes and symptoms of the disease. Increased awareness is the first step toward improved prevention strategies.

Diagnostic Techniques

Magnetic resonance imaging is undergoing constant refinement, and each step forward provides doctors with more accurate pictures of what is going on inside a patient's brain and arteries. The innovation of magnetic resonance spectroscopy is particularly interesting, because the new technology provides a profile of the most important brain chemicals and how they change during a stroke. Previous MRI scans showed only the physical structure of the brain and its chemical composition. If doctors wanted to probe a patient's brain chemistry, they would have had to operate to obtain a tissue sample. Magnetic resonance spectroscopy makes this invasive procedure unnecessary.

In addition, the new technology of functional magnetic resonance imaging (fMRI) will allow doctors to observe the brain more accurately while it is working and learn which parts of

A patient undergoes an fMRI scan, the latest diagnostic technology in the treatment of stroke.

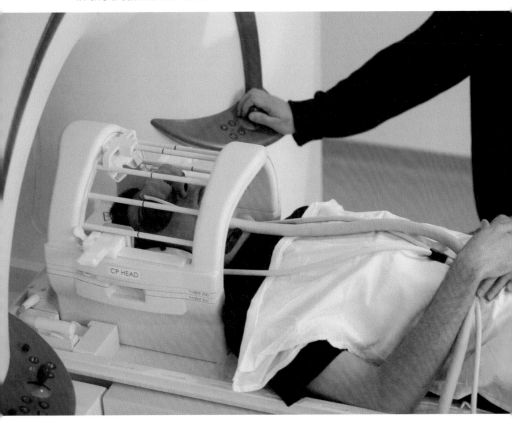

the organ are still functioning, which have been temporarily damaged, and which have been destroyed, thus enabling a more accurate prediction of the patient's potential for recovery and providing important guidelines for what forms of therapy should be stressed.

There are also other new scanning techniques on the horizon. Magnetic resonance angiography is an experimental procedure that creates images of the blood vessels in the brain and can detect very small abnormalities. Once fully operational, this tool will be valuable not only in diagnosing the patient's current condition but also in forecasting the likelihood of future problems so that doctors can intervene to correct them before they lead to another stroke. Xenon CT scanning will be able to chart blood flow and electrical activity in the brain, and carotid duplex scanning will provide the most accurate and detailed picture ever of the health of the carotid arteries and the location of a large number of stroke-causing blood clots. Positron emission tomography (PET) has yet to be perfected to the satisfaction of most doctors. The hope is, though, that this imaging tool will provide them with yet another way to look at how the brain is working without having to operate on the patient. PET is designed to detect very small interruptions in blood flow.

New Drugs

Impressive strides are being made in the development of drugs to treat stroke patients. The success of tissue plasminogen activator (tPA) has inspired the search for similar clot-dissolving drugs that have fewer adverse side effects and can be targeted more precisely at the area where the clot has occurred. One such drug, now undergoing clinical trials, appears to be successful if administered up to six hours after the onset of the stroke. That would expand the treatment window substantially.

New neuroprotective drugs are also being studied. These drugs will minimize the damage the brain endures during a stroke and will permit a greater number of brain cells to be saved. For example, several drugs that block the production of glutamate are in development. Glutamate is a chemical mes-

Herbal Medicine

Herbal remedies have been used in all parts of the world for centuries and still are in many societies. Industrialized nations have largely turned their backs on them because pharmaceutical drugs proved so effective. Recent experience has shown, however, that many pharmaceutical drugs have unwanted and serious side effects, and that has led to a renewed interest in herbal medicine.

In a recent study, the traditional Chinese herb gastrodine was pitted against the drug Duxila in a test to see which would best improve the memory in 120 stroke patients. The contest ended in a draw, with both the herb and the drug facilitating improved memory in 50 percent of the people who used it. However, the herb had fewer side effects.

Other herbs have demonstrated effectiveness in preventing stroke. These natural remedies include cayenne, goldenseal, and rose hip tea, all of which strengthen blood vessels and improve circulation. Silica, a substance contained in the herb horsetail, promotes elasticity of the arteries, and ginger reduces cholesterol, a leading cause of strokes.

senger in the brain, but when a stroke happens it can spill out of its proper channels and damage the surrounding tissue. Experimental drugs have shown the ability to block glutamate production after a stroke in animals; human trials are in the planning stages.

At the same time as researchers are working to improve drugs administered after a stroke, other scientists are perfecting medications that can help to prevent a stroke from happening in the first place. A new generation of anticoagulant drugs—drugs that inhibit the blood from clotting—holds out the promise that patients can be treated before they find themselves in a crisis. Similarly, breakthroughs in antiplatelet drugs will soon make it possible to prevent the accumulation of these clotting agents in the blood. Several drugs now under study are being tailored so they can be given to high-risk individuals before the onset of a first stroke, hopefully sparing them from a lifetime of disability. The American Stroke Association says that funding agencies are disbursing billions of dollars in research grants to promote the development of anticoagulant and antiplatelet drugs. This financial clout is reinforcing the new belief that the best way to attack strokes is to prevent them rather than attempt to deal with their consequences.

The goal of this new effort is to devise a two-pronged drug treatment that can even be given to ischemic stroke patients (85 percent of all strokes are ischemic) as soon as an MRI or other scan confirms they have not had a hemorrhagic stroke. One drug will break up the clot that is causing the stroke, and the other will protect the brain from damage. It is hoped that both functions will one day be combined in a single drug, further reducing the time between the beginning of a stroke and effective treatment.

Genetics

Genetics is revolutionizing all aspects of medicine, including stroke research. With the mapping of the human genome, it has become apparent that all aspects of life are governed, to some degree at least, by the genes inherited from parents. With this in mind, doctors are now paying more attention to family history to identify potential stroke victims before they suffer an attack. Noting a predisposition to stroke in a family, doctors can advise family members how to make lifestyle changes, improve diet and exercise habits, and possibly consider drug treatments to lower the risk of stroke.

Geneticists at the University of Texas Health Science Center in Houston have already pinpointed eleven genes that appear to play a role in inducing stroke in rats. "Ultimately, this project will apply the data from the experimental rat model to humans,"[45] says Dr. Mryiam Fornage. Fornage and other researchers are now sequencing the rat genes to determine which proteins that particular sequence of genes produces. Armed with that knowledge, they may one day be able to construct a drug that will deactivate the problem genes, dramatically reducing the number of people who are prone to stroke.

The University of Texas is engaged in an "all-out assault on the genetics of stroke," says Dr. Eric Boerwinkle, director of the Research Center for Human Genetics at the school's Institute of Molecular Medicine. "This includes family studies to map and identify stroke-susceptibility genes, animal model studies to examine gene expression in the brain, and clinical studies to identify genes that predict stroke risk."[46]

Rehabilitation Breakthroughs

While treatment of strokes is a primary concern, new conceptions of rehabilitation promise to give people who have had strokes a better chance than ever of regaining the abilities they lost to the attack. One example is the Supported Ambulation System, an innovative approach to physical therapy pioneered by Dr. Lester Dewis, director of the Stroke Program at Bryn Mawr Rehab in Malvern, Pensylvania. Patients relearn how to walk by being strapped into a parachute-like harness over a treadmill. As the patient's strength and balance begin to return, therapists gradually release the harness, putting progressively greater amounts of pressure on the patient's muscles. "In traditional rehab, the patients are taught how to do the best with what they've got—using their good limbs to compensate for the bad," Dewis says. "But with the method we're working on, which we call neurological therapy, we can make an arm or leg work again."[47]

Forced use therapy is another novel technique that attempts to reprogram the brain. Instead of teaching a stroke survivor to use unaffected limbs to compensate for lost mobility and motor function, therapists using this approach immobilize the patient's good limb and force him or her to use the weakened limb exclusively. Researchers at the Emory University and the University of Alabama have used imaging technology to show that forced use therapy enlists brain cells not normally used for mobility and limb function. The patient's brain actually undergoes physical changes in the region affected by the stroke as brain cells learn to play new roles.

Some of the proposed new therapies take a radical approach. One of the experimental treatments uses the botulism toxin, the most deadly substance known to science, to control muscle twitching in stroke victims. The botulism is administered directly into the muscle in a carefully controlled dose. It stops the release of a substance called acetylcholine, a chemical that

A stroke survivor uses the Supported Ambulation System during his rehabilitation sessions.

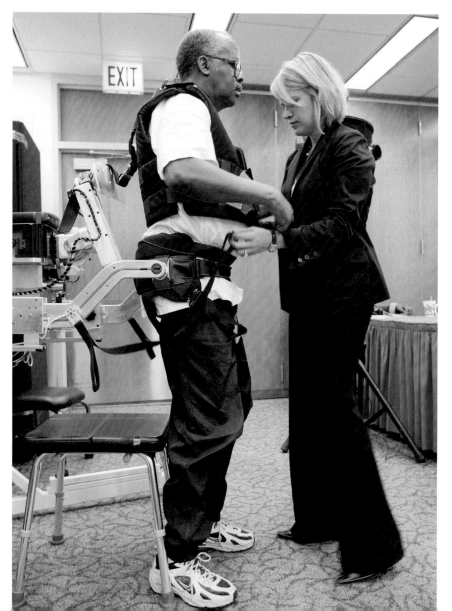

Bionic Revolution

Bionic implants are, for the first time, allowing stroke victims to regain the use of paralyzed or partially paralyzed limbs. In one case, electronic microstimulators were implanted into the right arm of forty-six-year-old Fran Read. She had been unable to use the arm since suffering a stroke eleven years earlier. During the intervening years, the muscles of the arm shrank and weakened considerably.

The stimulators are controlled by a radio-frequency cuff worn on the patient's arm. By pressing a button, she sends a signal to the bionic nerves in her arm, activating the muscles and allowing her to extend her elbow and open and close her fingers. Read's doctors at Southampton General Hospital in England hope that after using the device for three months, her brain will have re-learned how to move the muscles by itself and she will be able to discard her bionic helper.

---

stimulates nerve endings in muscles leading to the uncontrolled spasticity. The treatment works in about 90 percent of stroke patients, sometimes in as little as two weeks. The drug has yet to be approved by the Food and Drug Administration, but no adverse side effects have been reported in drug trials.

In some cases, therapies originally designed to treat other medical conditions are being used on stroke victims. Hyperbaric chambers, once confined to speeding the healing of wounds in other parts of the body, are being employed to help the brain heal itself following stroke. Hyperbaric chambers are routinely used to treat wounds by creating a high-oxygen environment that promotes healing. Brain scans administered to stroke patients before and after hyperbaric treatment show improved blood flow to the damaged parts of the brains and increased neurological activity in those areas. All participants in a study of the technique at the Galveston Transitional Learning Community in Texas have shown marked improvement.

Doctors and Patients

Perhaps the most important strides are being made in making sure stroke victims get timely and competent medical care. More and more cities are getting specialized stroke centers staffed by expert doctors and nurses. They provide state-of-the-art diagnostics and treatment. In the past, it was easy for less up-to-date hospitals to be designated as stroke centers, but thanks to a strident campaign by the American Stroke Association, many state governments have made the requirements far more stringent. To be called a primary stroke center, a facility must have adequate personnel and technology; to be called an advanced stroke center, it must have up-to-date technology and provide complete medical and surgical services.

Through telemedicine, this doctor can communicate with other remote physicians, providing immediate, specialized care to stroke victims.

Improved communications technology is also making it possible for doctors at one hospital to consult with specialists at another center. This is called telemedicine, and it enables patients to get quality, up-to-the-minute care no matter where they are. Patients in rural areas and small towns have not traditionally had access to the most fully qualified doctors in the stroke field. That is changing rapidly. Specialists at distant locations can examine the results of CT and MRI scans, render a definitive diagnosis, and guide the on-site physician in the most advanced treatment options.

Another positive trend that is expected to continue is the emphasis on prevention of stroke. Thanks to the American Stroke Association, the National Stroke Association, and other organizations, public awareness of stroke is increasing rapidly. Most experts agree that no matter how sophisticated medical science becomes at treating stroke, the surest line of defense is prevention.

The main problem on the horizon is cost. New diagnostic techniques and new treatment options are expensive. These technological advances will be available, but will society—the government and private insurance companies—be prepared to pay for them? The American Stroke Association and other advocacy groups are mounting a campaign to ensure that adequate funds will be available.

Although stroke is likely to remain a serious medical condition for millions of people in the foreseeable future, there is hope that advances in diagnosis and treatment will one day reduce the number of victims and limit the tragedy stroke causes in their lives and the lives of those who care for them.

Notes

Introduction: Sudden Tragedy
1. Quoted in Louis R. Caplan, *Stroke*. Saint Paul, MN: AAN, 2006, p. 1.

Chapter 1: What Is a Stroke?
2. Vladimir Hachinski and Larissa Hachinski, *Stroke: A Comprehensive Guide to Brain Attacks*. Buffalo, NY: Firefly, 2003, p. 3.
3. Quoted in The Franklin Institute, "The Human Brain." www.fi.edu/brain/carbs.htm.
4. Erica S., "A Stroke at 13," Bungalow Software. www. bungalowsoftware.com/info/stories/stroke_at_13.htm.
5. Erica S., "A Stroke at 13."
6. Erica S., "A Stroke at 13."
7. Debra, "With a Little Help from My Friends," Orgsites.com. www.orgsites.com/pa/_ppg6.php3.
8. Debra, "With a Little Help from My Friends."
9. Debra, "With a Little Help from My Friends."
10. Quoted in Marie McCain, "Felled by Stroke, Young Swimmer Fights to Recover," *Cincinnati Enquirer*, June 6, 1999. www.enquirer.com/editions/1999/06/26/loc_felled _by_stroke.html.
11. Quoted in McCain, "Felled by Stroke, Young Swimmer Fights to Recover."

Chapter 2: Symptoms and Diagnosis
12. Hachinski and Hachinski, *Stroke*, p. 39.
13. Edwin B. Jelks, "On Being Struck by a Stroke," Stroke Survivor. www.strokesurvivor.org/being_struck_2.htm.
14. Jelks, "On Being Struck by a Stroke."
15. Caplan, *Stroke*, p. 90.
16. Caplan, *Stroke*, p. 100.

Chapter 3: Treatment

17. American Stroke Association, "Tissue Plasminogen Activator (tPA)." www.strokeassociation.org/presenter.jhtml? identifier=4751.
18. Quoted in American Heart Association, "Studies Show the Need for Speed in Reacting to Stroke." www.scienceblog. com/community/older/2000/a/2000000505.html.
19. Quoted in American Heart Association, "Studies Show the Need for Speed in Reacting to Stroke."
20. Hachinski and Hachinski, *Stroke*, p. 47.
21. Caplan, *Stroke*, pp. 120–21.
22. Caplan, *Stroke*, pp. 136–37.
23. Hachinski and Hachinski, *Stroke*, p. 55.
24. Cleveland Clinic Health System, "Stroke Rehabilitation." www.cchs.net/health/health-info/0900/0900.asp?index= 5600.
25. Hachinski and Hachinski, *Stroke*, p. 60.

Chapter 4: Long-Term Care

26. National Stroke Association, "Rehabilitation Therapy." www.stroke.org/site/pageserver?pagename=rehabt.
27. The Patient Education Institute, "x-plain Stroke Rehabilitation: Reference Summary." www.x-plain.com.
28. George Jacob, "Paralysis or Problems Controlling Movement," Holistic Online.com. www.holisticonline.com/ REMEDIES/stroke_effects_disab_paralysis.htm.
29. Penny Montgomery-West, "A Spouse's Perspective on Life with Aphasia," National Aphasia Association. www.aphasia. org/article-pmwest.php.
30. Caplan, *Stroke*, p. 142.
31. Mark Tolley, "Which Vert Are You," Different Strokes, 2006. www.differentstrokes.co.uk.

Chapter 5: Prevention

32. American Stroke Association, "Stroke Risk Factors." www.strokeassociation.org/presenter.jhtml?identifier =4716.

33. Nina J. Solenski, "Transient Ischemic Attack: Part I. Diagnosis and Evaluation," American Academy of Family Physicians. www.aafp.org/20040401/1665.html.
34. Solenski, "Transient Ischemic Attack."
35. Peter Coleman and Stephen Davis, "Diabetes, Stroke and High Blood Glucose: A Recipe for Trouble," Diabetes Australia. www.diabetesaustralia.com.au/conquest/0301-diabetes-stroke.htm.
36. Hachinski and Hachinski, *Stroke*, p. 96.
37. P.B. Gorelick, "Stroke from Alcohol and Drug Abuse: A Current Social Peril," PubMed. www.ncbi.nim.nih.gov/entrez.
38. Stroke Association, "Alcohol and Stroke." www.stroke.org.uk/information/preventing_a_stroke/factsheets/alcohol_and.html.
39. Hachinski and Hachinski, *Stroke*, p. 100.
40. St. Luke's Episcopal Medical Systems, "Healthy Diet Can Help Prevent Stroke." www.sleh.com/sleh/section004/index.cfm?pagename=nutrition.
41. Stroke Association, "Diet and Stroke." www.stroke.org.uk/ information/preventing_a_stroke/factsheets/diet_and_stroke.html.
42. Angela Williams, "Exercises Lowers Stroke Risk," ABC Online. www.abc.net.au/health/thepulse/s1444090.htm.

Chapter 6: The Future

43. Hachinski and Hachinski, *Stroke*, p. 119.
44. Caplan, *Stroke*, p. 173.
45. Quoted in Scott Merville, "Decoding the Genetics of Brain Attack," Distinctions. www.uthouston.edu/distinctions/archive/2002/may/decoding_genetics.html.
46. Quoted in Barbara Alden Wilson, "Stroke: New Developments in Rehabilitation," Ivanhoe Broadcast News. www.search.invanhoe.com/archives/p_archive.cfm?stroyid=6274&channeled=chan-100013.

Glossary

aneurysm: A weak or thin bulge in the wall of a blood vessel that has a propensity to burst.

aphasia: The inability to speak, read, write, or understand language.

atherosclerosis: A hardening of the arteries due to the buildup of cholesterol-caused plaque.

blood pressure: The pressure exerted by the blood against the walls of the arteries.

brain stem: The part of the brain that links the two halves of the brain to the spinal column.

bruit: The telltale noise made by a partially blocked artery.

cardiovascular disease: Any disease that can affect the circulatory system. The term usually refers to coronary artery disease, heart failure, and stroke.

carotid artery: One of two large arteries running along the sides of the neck. The carotid artery is a principal supplier of blood to the brain.

cerebellum: The part of the brain that controls balance and coordination, among other functions.

cerebrum: The largest part of the brain. The cerebrum governs thought, language, and many other functions.

embolism: The blockage of a blood vessel by a blood clot originating in another part of the body.

hemorrhagic stroke: A stroke caused by a ruptured blood vessel, characterized by bleeding in the brain.

ischemic stroke: A stroke that occurs when an artery supplying the brain with blood becomes blocked by a clot or some other cause.

neurologist: A doctor specializing in the brain and nervous system.

plaque: A buildup of cholesterol and other fatty substances on the walls of arteries.

stroke: A sudden interruption of blood flow to the brain, caused by an obstruction in a blood vessel or the rupture of a blood vessel.

transient ischemic attack (TIA): A ministroke lasting less than twenty-four hours.

Organizations to Contact

American Stroke Association (ASA)
7272 Greenville Ave.
Dallas, TX 75231
(888) 478-7653
www.strokeassociation.org

The ASA is a fund-raising and advocacy organization that seeks to educate the public on strokes and reduce the risk of the disease. The ASA Web site provides information on all aspects of stroke, including special sections on warning signs, risk factors, information for caregivers, and how to prevent strokes.

National Stroke Associations (NSA)
9707 E. Easter Ln.
Englewood, CO 80112
(800) 787-6537
www.stroke.org

The NSA is an education and advocacy organization aimed at reducing the occurrence of stroke. The NSA Web site provides comprehensive information on strokes, with emphasis on therapy and coping strategies for survivors and their families. The site also carries news on the latest developments in stroke research.

Stroke Survivors International
www.strokesurvivors.org

Stroke Survivors International is a member organization that provides a clearinghouse of information and support for stroke survivors and their families. The organization's Web site carries medical information on stroke risk and treatments.

World Stroke Federation (WSF)
Department of Neurology
Upstate Medical University
750 E. Adams St.
Syracuse, NY 13210
(315) 492-5840
www.worldstrokefederation.org

The WSF is an informational organization that serves both professionals and the public. The WSF Web site is devoted to furthering research into the causes of stroke and developing new treatments for the disease. It contains links to other organizations as well as information on cutting-edge stroke research.

For Further Reading

Books

Ann Galperin, *Stroke and Heart Disease.* New York: Chelsea House, 1990. This book is aimed at younger readers and includes a reasonably complete description of the causes of stroke and the treatments available to the victims of this disease. It relates stroke to heart disease and other cardiovascular conditions and provides a good explanation of why problems develop in this field of medicine.

John R. Marler, *Stroke for Dummies.* Indianapolis, IN: Wiley, 2005. Written by a practicing neurologist, this book in a popular series explains strokes in uncomplicated terms and provides an excellent and easy-to-read overview of the subject, including information on prevention.

Richard Senelick and Karla Dougherty, *Living with Stroke: A Guide for Families.* Clifton Park, NY: Thomson Delmar Learning, 2001. This guide emphasizes the coping mechanisms available to the friends and loved ones of stroke victims. It describes the rehabilitation process in detail and discusses the principal causes of stroke.

Joel Stein, *Stroke and the Family: A New Guide.* Cambridge, MA: Harvard University Press, 2004. This book is part of a series of Harvard University Press Family Health Guides. It deals with all aspects of stroke—causes, treatment, and prevention—in a vocabulary that is easy to understand.

Barbara Toohey and June Biermann, *The Stroke Book: A Guide to Life After Stroke for Survivors and Those Who Care for Them.* New York: Tarcher, 2005. The authors, who are both experienced medical writers, focus on therapies and rehabilitation. They also provide a sympathetic assessment of the challenges recovery presents both to the stroke victims and their loved ones.

David Weibers, *Stroke-Free for Life: The Complete Guide to Stroke Prevention and Treatment*. New York: Harper-Collins, 2002. Weibers, a stroke specialist from the Mayo Clinic, offers a thorough explanation of stroke but concentrates on preventative measures and lifestyle.

Periodicals

Nicholas Bakalar, "Just Another Face in the Crowd, Indistinguishable Even If It's Your Own," *New York Times*, July 18, 2006. This article discusses prosopagnosia, a fascinating side effect of stroke. The condition is an inability to remember faces, even one's own when looking in a mirror.

Tamilyn Bakas, "Factors Associated with Hospital Arrival Time for Stroke Patients," *Journal of Neuroscience Nursing*, June 1, 2004. Although written for a scholarly journal, this article presents the procedures followed once a potential stroke victim arrives at a hospital from the unique perspective of the nurses who have to evaluate the patient's condition.

Cory SerVaas, "Stroke Victims Require Fast Care," *Saturday Evening Post*, August 2005. This report stresses the need for speed in reacting to stroke symptoms and lists the measures taken once the patient arrives at an emergency room.

Anne Walling, "How Critical Is Time in the Treatment of Stroke?" *American Family Physician*, January 1, 2005. The author reiterates the importance of an emergency room staff's ability to distinguish between ischemic and hemorrhagic stroke prior to the administration of clot-dissolving drugs. A failure to tell one type of stroke from another can put the patient's life at risk.

Web Sites

BBC Health: Strokes (www.bbc.co.uk/health/conditions/stroke). This site is maintained by the British Broadcasting Service, one of the world's leading news organizations. It discusses the nature of stroke, treatment, and prevention, and provides personal accounts of stroke victims.

Bon Secours Richmond Health System (http://healthlibrary. epnet. com). Written by a nurse who specializes in the treatment of stroke, this site includes complete information on the disease, including a concise definition, a discussion of causes and risk factors, a list of common symptoms, and two diagrams highlighting the difference between an ischemic and hemorrhagic stroke.

Medline Plus (www.nlm.nih.gov/medlineplus/stroke/html). This government site is maintained by the National Institutes of Health. It provides a wide range of information for the stroke researcher, including a special section for children.

Stroke Information Directory (www.stroke-info.com). This site contains a section on the latest breakthroughs in stroke treatment as well as general information on diagnosis and therapy. It also provides a glossary of relevant terms.

Index

Picture Credits

Cover photo: Zephyr/Photo Researchers, Inc.
Associated Press, 80
Maury Aaseng, 10, 13, 16, 25 (chart), 66
© Paul Barton/CORBIS, 30
Daniel Berehulak/Getty Images News/Getty Images, 88
John Cole/Photo Researchers, Inc., 19, 45
© CORBIS, 15
© Darama/CORBIS, 27
© Mark Harmel/Alamy, 81
© Jeremy Hogan/Alamy, 58
© Nucleus Medical Art, Inc./Alamy, 38
Scott Olson/Getty Images, 86
PhotoDisc, 7, 75
Photos.com, 25 (photo), 40, 64, 67
© Phototake Inc./Alamy, 34
James Prince/Photo Researchers, Inc., 49
© Katja Ruge/zefa/CORBIS, 73
© Chuck Savage/CORBIS, 77
© Norbert Schaefer/CORBIS, 61
Tom Stoddart/Hulton Archive/Getty Images, 44
David Young-Wolff/Stone/Getty Images, 51
Hattie Young/Photo Researchers, Inc., 52, 54
© Bo Zaunders/CORBIS, 70
Zephyr/Photo Researchers, Inc., 33

About the Author

Robert Taylor is a writer and editor who lives in Greenacres, Florida. His current interests include science, medicine, politics, philosophy, and mythology.